WAITING WITH PURPOSE

WAITING WITH PURPOSE

Persevering When God Says "Not Yet"

Jeannie Ewing

En Route Books & Media
5705 Rhodes Avenue, St. Louis, MO 63109
Contact us at contactus@enroutebooksandmedia.com

LCCN: 2017961387

Cover design by:
TJ Burdick
Cover image credits: Pixabay.com

Hardback ISBN: 978-0-9996670-0-2
Paperback ISBN: 978-0-9996670-1-9
E-book ISBN: 978-0-9996670-3-3

Printed in the United States of America

CONTENTS

FOREWORD

I despise waiting; it seems like so much wasted time. I guess I'm in good company; St. Teresa of Avila is said to have banged on her hourglass when the sand seemed to trickle through too slowly during her prayer time.

Doesn't our whole Western lifestyle seem to rail against stillness of any sort? We marinate in noise, apologize for saying no, multitask ourselves into inefficiency and burnout, berate the supermarket cashier when there's any line at all, and consider waiting a luxury or a silliness we cannot afford.

Or else we live at the other end of the spectrum and embrace laziness and excess as an entitlement. Let someone else kill themselves; I'll barely put forth the effort to do the job since I make the same salary either way. How much time can I waste and not get fired? How many resources can I squander in my mindless pursuit of entertainment? I deserve it.

Yet no one would say the "resources" or time spent by a seed in the soil or a baby in gestation are excessive or wasted, nor would anyone say that the seed or baby are lazy, however slowly or secretly they may pass. In fact, any interruption or prolonging of these processes would abnormally stunt the potential of the thing doing the "waiting."

This natural reality holds true in the spiritual realm too. The Israelites spent forty years in wilderness formation, getting to know God and learning how to worship Him properly so they could live well in their Promised Land. The number forty in the Bible is the number of gestation. Maybe it seemed like "wandering," but their waiting was active, living, and exact—as entitled as a baby in the womb.

In the scriptures, the more important a person's call from God, the longer it takes to make that person capable of receiving God's promise. The Israelites spent forty years in the wilderness because they were pioneering the formation of waiting for all of us. Joseph, Moses, and David all spent at least a grueling decade in the wilderness of formation. Abraham's call demanded twenty-five years, and once he received the promised son, God asked Abraham to give him back!

The apostles' formation time was shorter, but that seems to be because the potency of witnessing and participating in Jesus's Passion concentrated the process, as Jeannie so deftly points out in these pages.

In reading Jeannie's book, you might be struck—as I was—by the fact that Jesus not only ended His life in deliberate vulnerability but also began His life in the same patient, expectant helplessness. This punctuation at both ends of His doing seems designed to teach, and even warn, that neither the beginning nor the completion of life depends on us.

In my own formation, I received God's promise with excitement and set about making it happen. No waiting for me! God told me He wanted me to learn to rest, and I kept assuring Him I was not tired. No time to waste, Lord!

Jesus shows us that most of what we consider "life" is sandwiched between two periods of inactive helplessness—birth, or infancy, and death. Passion as dependence straddles human life. Helplessness, then, cannot be inferior to independence, as Jeannie emphasizes.

Resting, whether active or passive, is to wait well, to wait with purpose. Important matters are sorted out and gestating in every stillness. God knows we all have to *learn* how to wait with purpose. In *Waiting with Purpose*, Jeannie tells us how.

Sonja Corbitt
Author of *Unleashed, Fearless, Ignite,* and *Fulfilled*

INTRODUCTION

See, I am doing something new! Now it
springs forth, do you not perceive it?
In the wilderness I make a way, in the
wasteland, rivers.

—Isaiah 43:19

Waiting. The word often conjures images of disdain in our minds because—let's face it—no one likes to wait. We equate waiting with passivity, a sort of forced state of being in which we are victims of circumstance. "Wait it out," we hear matter-of-factly, and we respond with frustrated resignation. "You'll just have to wait" is another one we may have heard as children and still hear reverberating in our memories when life doesn't go as we anticipated.

As a naturally impatient person, waiting has always been a constant source of frustration for me. As a child, my family often reprimanded my impulsive and often brash reactions and responses with, "Don't be so bossy. People won't like you if you always speak your mind." My cheeks would flush in sweltering anger whenever an injustice occurred—either against me or against someone else. I didn't know how to temper such emotions, not then. Even today, it's tough.

I won't pretend that waiting God's way is easy, because it's not. But I've discovered, through my own experience and in understanding the spiritual opportunities that waiting often presents to us, that God remains faithful and brings to fruition the work He has begun in us. Sometimes that work is what we can clearly see and understand, but often it is not. One such example of waiting in my own life involves how I became an author.

As a child, my unspoken wish was to one day become a writer—a *real* writer, not just someone who wrote privately and had ambitions of seeing her byline in print! From the time I learned how to write well and realized that words could be connected in creative and beautiful phrases, I started keeping a journal. And I wrote in it daily.

I loved writing assignments at school because I could practice different forms of writing: prose, poetry, journalistic style, research, and creative writing. Poetry contests weren't off-limits, and I even won a citywide award that was sponsored by our county's library.

In fourth grade, my best friend and I decided to enter the Young Author's Conference and co-author a Nancy Drew-type book we entitled *The House on the Hill*. As two young girls with fresh and vivid imaginations, we wrote with alacrity on a daily basis instead of chatting idly about school and our friends and boys. We laughed and half-joked that one day we'd both write a teen fiction series called *Too Many Siblings, Too Many Pets*, and live on a horse ranch!

Essentially, we *worked*, and we worked *hard*. For me, it was one step closer to that burning desire to have my words read by people all over the world. I didn't realize how necessary the value of grit would be in determining how likely it would be that my dream would come alive, but I was a gritty gal when it came to writing. I may not have enjoyed cleaning my room, but I took writing seriously and practiced the craft every chance I had.

In college, I mastered the art of creating interesting and informative research papers rather than the drab missives of so many grad students. To me, writing in any form was a form of beauty and should be attractive to readers. It wasn't drudgery to me. It was pure bliss, a deep and abiding enjoyment.

Still, my major was not in creative writing, nor was it in editing or publishing or anything that had to do with fine arts. I majored in psychology and eventually school counseling. I suppose that's why writing was always a passion of mine: because it wasn't a career path, wasn't something I *had* to do. I did it for the sheer love of it. And that's what made me good at it.

Some might scratch their heads in bewilderment as to why I didn't opt to be an English or literature major. In so many words, I was told by various people that "no one makes any money as an author," so I should consider my alternatives. For me, the only alternative was psychology because I longed to understand more deeply how human behavior intersected with both a pathological and a healthy model of development.

So, I set aside my childhood aspiration and pursued something deemed more "practical" by societal standards. I don't regret it to this day, and here's why: my childhood dream eventually came true. But I had to travel a particular path that was very specific to getting to that long-forgotten reverie. God knew (of course) that I could not become a polished and credible author without years and years of private practice, as well as a hefty dose of life experience.

About twenty-five years after my stint at the Young Authors Conference with my best friend from grade school, our middle daughter, Sarah, was born. At the time, I was already a stay-at-home mom to our oldest daughter, Felicity, and I knew it was where I was meant to be. Though I often wondered why I donned two college diplomas in our upstairs guest room—one for my bachelor's and the other for my master's—I was at peace. I felt restless, as if there was more I should be doing, but I couldn't pinpoint what that was; that is, not until Sarah was born.

When Sarah arrived punctually, I was ready to meet her. But Ben and I were taken aback by her birth, which was incredibly dramatic, terrifying, and intense.[1] We loved her immediately, though we didn't truthfully know if she would live or die. Shortly after we brought her home, we learned that she was born with a rare genetic condition called Apert syndrome and would likely undergo between twenty and sixty surgeries throughout her life.

The subsequent two weeks postpartum were sheer agony for me. I was engulfed in a thick darkness, one that spiraled me into a place bordering on embitterment. I often sobbed to God, pleaded with Him, and even screamed when I was all alone downstairs at night. In His great mercy, He opened my heart and my eyes to unveil the truth that I was embarking on a potentially dangerous journey. One night, He spoke softly to my heart: "You can choose victimhood or victory, but you cannot have victory without the Cross."

I chose to walk with Jesus through the crucible of suffering by way of raising a daughter with a lifelong condition that would require an immense amount of time, energy, and money on the part of our family. And once I made that choice, I knew I had to do something fruitful, something tangible and meaningful, with this new way of life and the mélange of emotions that I couldn't seem to sort through rationally.

So, I prayed. I asked the Lord what He wanted me to do, and His answer was, "Write." Remember, I had been writing privately for decades and had only been trivially published sporadically up until that point. So the call to write didn't seem new to me—only it was. It was a call to start writing visibly, and that began with a blog to share our journey with Sarah's rare disease.

This quickly grew to blogging for one Catholic website, then another, then still more. I wrote gratis because I was just obeying what God had asked of me, but there was a burning restlessness in my soul that I couldn't shake. In spiritual direction, I discerned that I was called to write a book, but about what? And how? I had virtually *no iota* of experience in the culture of crafting a book proposal, query letter, even writing an outline of a book or researching which publishing companies might be a good fit.

So, I waited, but I did so reluctantly and passively, not in joy, not in trust, and certainly not patiently. I didn't share this insight with anyone, except my husband Ben and my spiritual director, but I prayed every day, and I did so fervently and persistently. For several months, the call to write a book grew stronger in me, but I didn't understand how it would come about or even where to begin.

Then I received an email from my editor at one of the online Catholic forums I regularly contributed to. He asked me if I had ever considered writing a book, because he noticed a thematic element to my articles and mentioned that they really resonated with the audience. He felt I should compile a book on the subject, and guess what it was? Grief.

I didn't want to write about grief at all, because it's such an intense and difficult topic to tackle. But I saw this email, prayed and waited several more months, and just hoped that something would fall into place at the proper time. One day, as I was on the cusp of giving up the idea altogether, I received a random phone call from a friend whom I'd only spoken with on the phone but never met in person. She said, "I was praying for you today, Jeannie, and you're supposed to write a book called *From Grief to Grace.*"

Taken aback, I thanked her and hung up the phone, my mouth gaping at nothing and no one. Fear and panic swept in. What would this look like? Why now? I didn't see at the time that writing wasn't just an avocation for me; it was clearly a true vocation, or a call-within-a-call. That was sobering, but it woke me up and had me thinking more deeply and profoundly about the possibility of where God was leading me.

Again, out of obedience, I drafted a crude non-fiction book proposal and swiftly sent it to my editor, who then submitted it to the publisher he knew. I waited but had no expectation of a specific outcome. I just prayed.

Weeks passed, and I hadn't thought much about the book proposal. From what I had learned, potential authors can wait for months without hearing a yay or nay from a prospective publishing company. Expecting this, I hung on to hope, and strangely, my interior peace did not waver during that season of waiting. It was excruciating on one hand, but on the other, I had this incredible and sublime confidence that God was in control of this.

Then, one blustery but sunny January morning, as I was driving home from dropping off Felicity at preschool, it hit me: They are going to accept my book proposal. It was so clear to me that I would've never doubted its veracity. Sure enough, an email from the publisher was waiting for me when I returned home that said, "We love your book idea and would like to offer you a contract."

Stupefied, I realized that this was God's plan. It had to be. All at once, everything made sense: the burgeoning interest in dabbling with creative writing as a kid, practicing without any clear purpose or intention as I grew older, and then going through college to be educated on an entirely different subject area. It was so that God's hand would be evident when this fell into place, and it was a dream I had set aside for so long that I truly didn't think it would ever fall into place.

But God was preparing me and pruning me for all those decades. He asked me to wait, at times without me even realizing what I was waiting for. He planted that desire to become a published author in my heart. And it was God who nurtured that longing throughout my formative years, adolescence, and early young adulthood. I just didn't see it, because it wasn't the appointed time yet. Love had not yet blossomed, because it wasn't mature enough—not until Sarah had entered the world and my faith had been tested more than ever before.

At that point, I saw that God was asking me to live what I was called to write about. That's a tough expectation. But God, in His vast wisdom, knows when we need to wait and for how long. And He always, always has a grander plan for us than our loftiest goals. As a ten-year-old giddy daydreamer, I couldn't have fathomed that one day I would be a book author who wrote about subjects that often slip through the crevices of the world's taste for beauty. But my calling—like yours—is to know with such incredible faith that God is *always* good and *always* brings about a greater good than what our trials of waiting seem. Waiting seems nebulous and sometimes nefarious, but we can cling to the theological virtue of hope when waiting is a mystery. Hope tells us not to give up, to in fact persevere, and to look to the horizon where the fulfillment of God's promise awaits us.

Most of us want life to happen now, and we are fortunate (or perhaps unfortunate) that almost everything we want or need *can* happen now. Thanks to our Information Age, everything is at our disposal in seconds—purchasing retail online, Googling informative or interesting facts, finding song lyrics, paying bills, communicating with someone across the globe, and on and on. Instant gratification has become our nemesis in a way, because it has trained us that waiting is fruitless and a waste of time, when in fact, waiting presents countless opportunities for us to grow.

Somehow, by God's grace, I decided I would use my time fruitfully. I wanted to see the world and appreciate the grandeur and beauty it had to offer, because I knew God didn't want me to shrivel away into a pile of dust before my life had truly begun.

Friends, life is mostly about waiting, isn't it? It's not about living foolishly or impetuously. It's not about constantly being a go-getter or pushing our way to the top of the corporate ladder. It's about how we respond to the lulls in our lives, the periods of time when nothing seems to be moving forward, at least not how we'd prefer. We can choose to be passive victims of these unexpected situations, like I initially did with becoming a published author, or we can allow God to work within us, to change us from within, while we wait for Him to honor His promise in our lives.

Looking in retrospect, even as I retell this story to you, I realize how petulant my longings were in my childhood. True to my melancholic nature, I erroneously believed that my life was wasting away and I'd never reach my lofty goal of becoming a published writer. I didn't fully embrace the time I was given to fulfill other dreams I'd stored somewhere latent in my heart—the dream to travel, to create, to serve.

Surprises will befall us. We will experience spurts and even long droughts of spiritual aridity. Sometimes we make plans, and those plans effortlessly fall into place. But sometimes our plans are interrupted by death, divorce, or disease. Sometimes God says to us, "Not yet, my darling, not yet." And sometimes waiting entails total surrender on our part so that His plan will come to pass in our lives. No matter, waiting means that God wants something great for us, often greater than our biggest plans and dreams.

Are any of us fully capable of envisioning God's entire plan for our lives? Do we truly see the newness that springs forth from desolation and heartache? No, of course not. No one is able to foresee the infinitely wise plans of God, and perhaps

He brings about something new and beautiful—the waters in the wastelands of our lives—from our pain, from our waiting.

We have to be willing to allow the "not yet" to become a seed that germinates in us for however long it takes for us to be ready for what's to come. Many times this will entail suffering and sacrifice on our part, and certainly it will include pruning of our vices, bad habits, and even undesirable personality traits. But waiting, friends, can be a time of watchful anticipation, of rest and rejuvenation. And it can produce in us spiritual fruits and virtues that fortify us for the time when that seed, perhaps planted so long ago, becomes a young flower, budding and ready to unfurl.

In this book, we will journey together through this spiritually fruitful aspect of our lives that we call waiting. We will explore how the Israelites and Moses experienced waiting differently, as well as what happened to Jesus during his forty days in the desert, and temptations we can expect to encounter along our own desert waiting. We will learn about hidden opportunities of waiting, the importance of rest, and overcoming missional loneliness through Scripture and spiritual writers who discovered long ago what you and I are now discovering together—that waiting is God's gift to us, and we must unwrap it only when He reveals the time. As the lovely line in Song of Songs says, "Do not rouse, do not stir up love before its time" (Song 2:7).

Chapter One

Why is Waiting So Difficult?

Enter into the land of mystery,
the land of vision!

—Archbishop Luis M. Martinez,
Worshipping a Hidden God

I hate winter, which is unfortunate and ironic, considering the fact that I live in north central Indiana. We enjoy about four months of temperate weather each year. The rest of the time? Ice, snow, sleet, freezing rain, grey skies—you get the idea. Somehow the long nights and short hours of daylight during those blustery and dreary winter months make me want to hibernate, and I can't help but wonder why I've so often squandered winter rather than enjoy what it has to offer me.

Winter is the perfect analogy for waiting, because it is a season of rest, solitude, and slow growth. It contrasts the abundance of summer, with its many hours of daylight, ample sunshine, and plentiful fruits, vegetables, and flowers. Winter reminds us that waiting, though painful and often clandestine, reveals something beautiful within us if we allow the seed of patience and perseverance to germinate.

It seems that summer suits most of us, doesn't it? Most of us are accustomed to running ourselves ragged, driving all over creation, and feeling as if we can't keep up with the pace of life. That frenzied lifestyle is something we are not only used to, but it might even be something we enjoy. It's easier to get tasks accomplished with efficiency if we keep moving without stopping.

But periods of waiting offer us a different perspective on life. Like winter, the lulls in our lives might indicate wiser ways of living, perhaps with more appreciation of the little gifts and blessings, perhaps more intentionally than habitually. Our relationships deepen, much as roots deepen beneath the surface of frozen ground, when we invest our most treasured asset—our time.

SOCIETAL PERSPECTIVES AND INFLUENCES ON WAITING

Why, then, is waiting so tough for most of us who aren't naturally inclined toward patience, silence, and solitude? It seems there are several factors at play, namely frenetic intemperance, acedia, and the culture of impatience that defines our Information Age.

To begin, "frenetic intemperance" is a term coined by author John Horvat II, which he defines as "a restless, explosive, and relentless drive inside man that manifests itself in modern economy by 1) seeking to throw off legitimate restraints; and 2) gratifying disordered passions."[2] All of us have witnessed scenes of explosive behavior when we're out and about. I tend to see it most often when I am driving. The recklessness and road rage that often leave me gripping the steering wheel and reciting the Rosary aloud are enough to rattle anyone these days. But there's so much more to frenetic intemperance, isn't there?

It seems to be an undercurrent that drives who we are in the Western World and what we do. Standing in line at the grocery store for more than five minutes? You'll see frowns and hear deep sighs and maybe impatient comments muttered by customers, and the general sense is one of tension and a "hurry up" attitude that leaves even the most well-intentioned of us frazzled.

Take a peek at the consumerist mindset that fuels many people's disordered passions. I think about how technology is constantly changing, to the point where I feel like I've just become acquainted with a particular software update when another one pops up on my computer. Even computers themselves become obsolete after only a few months or so on the market. At times, I've lamented to Ben that I simply can't keep up with the latest digital devices, the apps, or their features; and everything online seems to scream at me, "Faster! Bigger! Better!"

So this, friends, is just a smidgen of a sample of what frenetic intemperance looks like. We all can come up with our own examples and understanding of how we've experienced it. And, to be perfectly honest, none of us are immune to falling prey to the frenzied pace of life. We have all become victims of our culture to some degree or another, whether or not we try to avoid the latest and greatest gadgets, a harried and hurried daily schedule, etc. In fact, many times we cannot avoid what's on our calendars, because it's been decided for us—by bosses, coaches, teachers, ministry leaders, and so on.

The point is: *there's always something going on, and we tend to get upset about what we can't control.* And that's a problem, because it trains our brains and bodies to be on the go constantly and without respite. When we come to plateaus in our lives where we actually have a moment to breathe, our natural response is to panic. Because, after all, we're supposed to be doing something, right? Something must be awry if we aren't moving with the societal current to which we've become accustomed.

Acedia and impatience are the spiritual counterparts to frenetic intemperance. Where frenetic intemperance tends to do more with the economic and political climate of our epoch, acedia is the spiritual cause, and impatience the fruit of such lifestyles. To be clear, acedia is considered "spiritual sloth," but it is really the flipside of the vice of sloth. In other words, we tend to think of sloth as being lazy and spiritually apathetic, which is true.

Theologically, we can define acedia as the "despair from weakness" or "the despairing refusal to be oneself."[3] What does that mean exactly? How can a person despair over his weakness or by denying himself to be authentic? Apparently, acedia is a type of spiritual sadness, a refusal or denial of our eternal destiny. Discovering that authentic living requires intentionality in striving for Heaven can be quite saddening to a soul who is not ready or willing to give Himself to the Lord. That is at the root of acedia, or spiritual sloth.

But acedia also includes over-commitment to our calendars and being so busy that we are not spiritually disciplined to spend a dedicated amount of time in prayer and reflection. That's how sloth can play out in our lives: through overt sins of omission, or through a more cunning and subtle form of busyness that appears to be good, when in fact it is leading us further away from God.

Impatience, of course, is the result of both acedia and frenetic intemperance. Time never seems to be on our side, so we often feel flustered and restless that we haven't accomplished everything we set out to do—or all that our bosses, family members, or friends expect us to do. In turn, we become irritable and follow the chaos and upheaval of the world around us. Impatience breeds anger, which often erupts in ugly ways.

The opposite of acedia isn't necessarily working our noses to the grindstone, so to speak. Rather, it is a very deliberate, joyful "affirmation of [our] own being, [our] acquiescence in the world and in God—which is to say, *love*."[4] We will discover throughout this book how waiting unfolds in our personal journey to a place of living this type of love—a freedom or liberation from the restraints of despair into a place of intentional happiness and purpose.

In his critically acclaimed classic, *The Stature of Waiting*, W. H. Vanstone explains why our modern world is constantly buzzing with this frenetic intemperance and the primary reason for our response to it: "Frustration…is caused not so much by the occasional failure of systems as by the constant necessity of waiting upon them. Frustration begins in awareness of oneself as waiting of necessity on factors beyond one's control…in general, this awareness gives rise to dissatisfaction, anger, and resentment."[5]

Waiting, then, can and often does draw us to a more astute awareness of who we are, what we need, and the needs of others around us. If we ignore this awareness or turn an apathetic heart toward it, we are likely to respond to waiting with the fear, anger, resentment, and impatience that is often evident.

Waiting, therefore, isn't always about wishing or hoping that something we want will come about in time, even in God's time. It's true that God begins His work in us, and sometimes we know what that work is, but often we don't. At least, we don't fully comprehend the greater picture of what He wants to accomplish in our lives. And that is why waiting is so arduous. We wait in joyful hope, but we may end up disappointed if our dreams come crashing down.

Here's a case in point: I know plenty of couples who have prayed and longed for children, yet they have remained childless. Why? One might assume that their waiting would produce biological children, simply because they believe it is God's will. But perhaps the burning desire for children—while truly planted by God—is to come to fruition by way of adoption, fostering children, or even acting as spiritual parents through mission work.

We don't want to become complacent in our waiting, nor do we want to be presumptuous. Many societal factors influence how we wait, so we are constantly battling the world and its temptations for us to give up, decrease in zeal, lose our luster in faith, and ultimately succumb to despair and bitterness. But God doesn't want us to forget about Him or turn our backs on Him simply because He asks us to hold on for a time while He works in our hearts and lives in ways we don't fully understand. Why has the world forgotten about God, and how can we ensure that we do not give up when our longings do not come to pass?

After exploring the philosophy of why waiting is difficult for most of us, we will delve more deeply into the active and passive states of waiting, which offer two divergent ways we wait for and on God to act in our lives.

Here's another perspective, written by Cardinal Robert Sarah, about why the world has forgotten about God. It is safe to say that we live in what he terms a "Godless society." Godlessness, unfortunately, runs rampant in nearly every facet of our culture:

A Godless society, which considers any spiritual questions a dead letter, masks the emptiness of its materialism by killing time so as better to forget eternity. The farther material things extend their influence, the more man takes pleasure in sophisticated, narcissistic, and perverse amusements; the more man forgets God, the more he observes himself.

In looking at himself, he sees the deformations and the ugliness that his debauchery has encrusted on his face.[6]

The point here, then, is that acedia—excessive busyness, concern with "sophisticated" matters of acquiring material wealth, and a narcissistic concern with self—contributes to all sorts of reasons why waiting is distasteful. It is seen as the antithesis of pleasure, and when we indulge in pleasure, we entirely forget about God and the purpose of our existence, which is to know, love, and serve Him wholeheartedly.

The origins of such beliefs can be found in the early Greek philosophers, who philosophized that work was the highest good man could seek and achieve. Once St. Thomas Aquinas studied Aristotle and Plato, however, he differentiated between "meritorious" work and work that is viewed as an end to itself. In other words, Aquinas incorporated a Christian worldview into the philosophy of work; he encouraged others to see work as valuable *only* if it has virtue attached to it. Likewise, the state of "not working," or simply being, he believed can also be worthwhile if it is spent in a state of receiving the beauty, gifts, and wonder that God has bestowed upon us.[7]

So we can clearly see how waiting is incompatible with a secular lifestyle when it comes to spiritual discipline and necessity for growth in our relationships with others. God offers it to us as a gift, as a way for us to recuperate from killing our bodies and our souls with the poison of busyness, but we so often squander the gift of time by filling it with forms of escapism and other distractions. We tend to think that doing rather than being is what matters most.

Perhaps the biggest reason waiting is a constant struggle is that our perspective of what waiting is depends largely upon the societal perspective that doing (e.g., working or being productive and independent) is of greater value to our inherent dignity as persons than is being (e.g., what is done to us, how others may love or help us). Vanstone believes that "waiting, from a Christian viewpoint, is never a degraded condition, a condition of diminished human dignity."[8] If this is true, then we must begin to change our attitudes and perceptions of waiting's purpose in our lives.

Desert Waiting

If we think about it more deeply, God gave us plenty of examples of why waiting is so crucial for our interior lives. As a Christian, I like to look at waiting in light of Scripture. In this light, we find examples of what may be called "desert waiting." The journey of Moses and the Israelites, as well as Jesus's forty days spent alone in the desert, are two such examples that belie the societal perception that doing trumps being. In the midst of desert experiences, we learn about the struggles that often lay hidden as we traverse to that place of emptiness and solitude.

Let's be honest: desert waiting is really tough. And it requires a particular level of resolve to muddle through the temptations and trials that most certainly await us when life, especially our spiritual life, becomes arid rather than temperate. To better understand how the desert experience relates to our understanding of waiting, we can reflect on how Moses, the Israelites, and Jesus handled the struggles they encountered on their long journeys through the wilderness.

During the exodus from Egypt, the Israelites were initially jubilant about being freed from enslavement. Generations of toil without reprieve wore down their bodies and their faith. Many were devout Hebrews who knew that God promised to deliver them, but many had forgotten or become too weary from the daily oppression that bogged them down. When Moses answered the call to free his people, the skeptics among the Israelites soon became believers once they saw the many wonders God performed through Moses.

All of us enter into periods of waiting with earnest anticipation. Perhaps we're looking forward to some quiet time or a chance to stay indoors and sleep a bit more. At first, we are much like the Israelites: eager, grateful, and ready for the change of pace. Yet, after a while, perhaps a few days or maybe even weeks or months of waiting, we become restless and might start grumbling to God.

That's exactly how the Israelites responded, and who could really blame them? They wandered seemingly aimlessly in the desert for forty years without knowing when or where they'd eventually settle down to permanently reside. They complained to Moses often, sometimes about how life in Egypt was better than roaming in the desert, and sometimes about how they'd become tired of their heavenly food of manna and quail.

Despite the fact that Moses interceded for them, the consequences of their grousing was a direct result of their lack of trust in God. Aren't we also like that? If God invites us into a period of time in which we may see little to no progress in our careers, our family situation, our finances, or our personal growth, we might start to lose trust in Him, too. Human nature becomes fickle when we cannot see what is in store for our future. We might once have carried a resounding zeal and faith in God, but it becomes lackluster over time when there is no indication of change.

How tragic, too, that the Israelites wasted their opportunity in the desert through griping and whining, like small children. God never failed them; He always provided for their temporal and spiritual needs. Instead of focusing on gratitude for His provident care, they continued to look back to the fine foods they enjoyed while enduring enslavement in Egypt, or they kept questioning what lay ahead for them in the future and when the waiting would cease.

We are a lot that way—frequently lamenting the past or peering too far ahead into the future instead of valuing the gift of this present moment. During times of waiting, we may falter from a present-moment focus because of our restlessness, our longing for answers, or the comfort of controlling what we understand. But God asks us to trust and abandon the questions into the mystery of the unknown. It is only during the unknown periods of waiting when we can grow in trust and abandonment, and we see time and again how God will never fail to provide for all that we need.

Father Peter John Cameron, O.P. defines this beautifully in the *Magnificat* periodical: "For forty years the Israelites wandered in the desert. The Lord led them in their lengthy vigil, preparing them to enter into the Promised Land. Never did they go without food, without water, without protection. God's calendar and schedule are not our own. We wait in faith. We follow as disciples. We rejoice in the way God's will unfolds."[9]

So, you see, we do not wait in vain, even and especially in the desert. We must remain faithful to the Lord's call, even if it may entail months or years of solitude and wandering without any change in sight. Faith requires that we embrace what we cannot yet see, which then transforms us into a hopeful, rather than despondent, people.

Moses, however, obeyed God and continued leading the Israelites through their desert journey until they finally reached the Promised Land. And once he beheld the beauty and fulfillment of what God promised to His people, Moses died. Wouldn't it be spectacular to catch a glimpse of a fulfilled promise, even if we never have the chance to enjoy it? I think of the countless saints who spent many years, decades even, in their own interior deserts. Some were privileged to enjoy the fruits of their fidelity to God, while others only saw God's plan come together on the horizon. If we only persevered through the droughts of our lives, which often affect every facet of our existence—physical, emotional, and spiritual—then perhaps we, too, might die in gratitude for knowing that the journey was worthwhile.

Father Tadeusz Dajczer explains the desert as "only a path" and "not a dwelling place."

> A desert experience is a time when a person becomes formed according to the rule that only what is difficult and gives resistance molds a person. The love of God, which is then born in you, should finally become communion with God.[10]

The desert, though barren and seemingly fruitless, holds a promise for the soul whose faith is unwavering and remains steadfastly resolved to follow God's plan through the nothingness. The desert, necessary for every soul, prepares it for the fulfillment of the promise, just as Moses believed in arriving at the Promised Land. We can remain steadfast in our spiritual aridity, knowing it is only transitory and not permanent—a path and not a dwelling place.

One potentially fruitful aspect of the soul's desolation is its formation of obscure faith, which we will discuss in more detail later in the book. Obscure faith reveals truth to the soul; its weaknesses indicate a total reliance on God, a complete surrender and dependence on Him for mercy and redemption.

The desert's spiritual dryness does not comfort and console. It is tasteless, unappealing, and bereft of color or bounty. The soul cannot behold beauty within itself; instead, only darkness and emptiness envelop the soul. If its faith is strong, it will turn to God with humility and thank Him for delivering it into the hands and heart of mercy.

So God's mercy is really at the heart of our desert moments of waiting in life. Barrenness of the soul is really a reflection of the reality that we can do nothing beneficial apart from God. If the soul has nothing in and of itself to offer God, this condescension leads it to seek the fullness and perfection that is in God alone. And once the soul discovers God in the desert, it is profoundly grateful for such a treasure. Nothing else satisfies the soul, except God alone.

Desert waiting often carries this deep spiritual significance for us, particularly when God has called us to fulfill a specific mission or purpose. Greatness is born of the struggle of spiritual aridity, testing, and temptation, though we seldom see the dry spells of life that way. Many of us give up altogether after a period of time, because we cannot believe in what we do not see. Our faith is perhaps tied to our senses rather than to authentic trust in the One who never fails us.

Spiritual aridity also refines virtues that we may lack and plucks out vices that may be habitual obstacles to whatever God has planned for us. The key is faithfulness and perseverance, but both are not so easily practiced.

Consider the verse, "Thy word is a lamp unto my feet and a light unto my path" (Psalm 119:105). There have been many aspects of my own desert journey in which I cannot see anything at all happening in my life, though others may notice incredible growth or tremendous spiritual fruits manifested through my relationships and writing. During the moments when my faith begins to falter and I start to stumble on the path to doubt and despair, I remember this verse, which reminds me that God reveals His light *one step at a time*.

That's truly the key to perseverance and remaining faithful to what God asks of us in dry spells and dark nights: visualizing our steps in darkness, revealed only one at a time by the One who knows the big picture. And when the waiting becomes just too intense for us to bear (seemingly) alone, we remember Jesus's journey in the desert for forty days and how He walks with us in our own spiritual aridity.

In her book *Fearless*, Sonja Corbitt shares, "The children of Israel teach us that the desert can be a barren place of great temptation and fear. But from Jesus we learn the desert can also be a place of purposeful isolation and the removal of distractions, a place of calling and mission, and great graces."[11] We will explore each of these aspects of temptation and fear (chapter 4) and how waiting leads us to our passion, which is the fulfillment of our ultimate mission on earth (chapter 5). For now, let's delve into Jesus's desert experience and what that can teach us about the beauty and value of our own desert waiting.

Shortly following His baptism, Jesus isolated Himself into the Judean desert, where He fasted and prayed for forty days and forty nights in preparation for the work that lay ahead. This was before He was commissioned by the Father to His public ministry, which is of great significance to those of us who feel as if we have been "waiting on the sidelines," so to speak, for our own purpose to be revealed or fulfilled by God. The synoptic Gospels recount Jesus's desert waiting, in which He encountered Satan and experienced three distinct temptations: for food, power, and wealth.

In our current era, most of us have been tempted in a literal sense for each of these enticements, but the spiritual symbolism of each temptation has great value to those of us who are in the midst of our own desert waiting. The fact that Jesus knew He must be prepared for His work on earth through the gift that awaited Him in the wilderness demonstrates to us that the desert prepares us for what is to come—*something more, something greater than where we are right now*. We may feel stagnant in any area of our life, but if we enter into the aridity with confidence in God's timing, He will accomplish great things in and through us.

When Satan approached Jesus with the temptation to turn the stones into loaves of bread, He knew Jesus was ravenously hungry since He had been fasting for weeks. We, too, can look at our own hunger, perhaps a spiritual hunger or longing that has yet to be completed in us. Fasting, which is a form of spiritual poverty, may teach us how to persevere through the initially painful pruning of waiting. Fasting is where we enter our desert journey, alongside Jesus, and ask Him: "What do you want from me, Lord? How can I sacrifice more of myself and my desires for your greater glory and honor?"

Fasting, of course, does not have to be merely from food; it can include an array of ways you may find God asking you to strip yourself of attachments: from the internet or technology, your favorite TV show, gaming, drinking alcohol, a particular vice (talking too much without listening, for example), etc. The point is, when we take that first step into the wilderness with Jesus, we are reminded that "man does not live by bread alone" (Matthew 4:4).

Jesus's second encounter with the devil involved the enticement for power (which, of course, Jesus already had the fullness of). Satan mocked Jesus's divinity by saying, "If you are the Son of God, you can fall off of this mountaintop and the angels will come to your aid." Though I am greatly paraphrasing here, it's important to note that the devil used Scripture verses in the temptations in order to make the temptations more appealing or to mask them as truth. Jesus's response was, "It also is written, 'You shall not put the Lord your God to the test'" (Matthew 4:7).

As we wander more deeply into our own wilderness, we must ask ourselves: *Are we willing to wait for God to reveal our missional identity in His time and way?* Sometimes we are inclined to forge ahead with an idea or goal impulsively and impetuously, but the second temptation of Christ grounds us in the truth that waiting for the proper time of fulfillment supersedes our own desire to step ahead of the difficulty we encounter in the arid loneliness of desert waiting.

The final temptation of Jesus culminated with Satan offering to give Jesus all the money and riches of every earthly kingdom in exchange for Jesus worshipping him. At first glance, we might assume that this temptation, of all of them, is of little consequence; but remember that this was toward the conclusion of Jesus's forty days and nights in the desert, after He had been stripped of all worldly comforts and spiritual consolations. Jesus, placing his trust as always in the Father, responded quickly, "Get away, Satan! For it is written, 'You shall worship the Lord God and it is Him alone you shall serve'" (Matthew 4:10).

Once the devil fled from Jesus, the angels immediately came to Jesus's aid for consolation and encouragement. It was through the three temptations of Christ that Jesus's power was most wonderfully made manifest. In our times of weakness and trial, we too can rest in the assurance that God may be glorified through our fidelity to His leadings and beckoning, even and especially when they lead us to what seems like nothing.

The third temptation begs the question for us: Are we allured to forego our passion, sacrifices, and suffering in the midst of this intermittence of waiting? What suffering may be necessary for the fulfillment of God's promises? Often, the temptations become more intense shortly before a spiritual breakthrough occurs. In other words, Satan tries more forcefully to bring us to despair or sin in some other way right before God calls us out of a period of waiting and into a springtime of fulfillment.

At this point, we may ask ourselves, "What's the point of all of this? Why can't I just bypass any sort of wilderness experience and get straight to the heart of my calling in life?" Consider the possibility, dear friends, that your calling might require so much more than you believe it does. It may be so grand, so beautiful, that you must be rightfully and fully prepared—through the wisdom of the desert trials—to accept the challenges, persevere through the persecution, and have the courage to face your fears only by way of what the desert can teach you.

Sonja Corbitt beautifully and aptly shares a point that draws home the message of Moses and the Israelites, as well as Jesus's desert experience: "The Holy Spirit leads us to the desert to empty us of Egypt so he can fill us with the promise of himself. In God's plan, the desert is a time to engage in ascetical practices. We need the desert to teach us to be fearless so we can advance in confidence."[12]

So, you see, the desert may be void of the life to which we are accustomed.

The desert entails harsh winds; sand storms; hot, dry days; and cold, dark nights; and it does not reveal what lies ahead for us. Day after day, we encounter what appears to be an empty wasteland—the nothingness, the lack of response or warmth from God, no indication of progress in our interior lives or otherwise. It is a place of dirt and dust, of barrenness and forsaken land.

But that is what our immediate perception would have us believe, isn't it? The desert, in fact, is a place in our lives where greatness blossoms, but only over time and through careful pruning and purgation. Though it's apparently a barren wilderness with no signs of hope or life, we can discover the hidden springs and oases that offer temporary refreshment from the heat of the refiner's fire. If we lean into the desert rather than flee from it, we will learn the riches of wisdom that are latent and waiting for us to discover.

THE CONSOLATION OF DESOLATION

When we've been in a place of desert waiting for a time, we begin to appreciate St. John of the Cross's concept of the dark night of the soul. Holy darkness draws us away from ourselves and the world and into the deeper recesses of our hearts, where we seek God. As we search for Him (which we'll discuss more in Chapter 2), our senses are often darkened. We cannot understand why God would withdraw Himself from us. But has He?

Truthfully, God often shields us from feelings, especially as we grow spiritually, because the more closely united we are with Him, the more terrifying and crucifying those feelings would be to us. So the darkness, therefore, is actually a blessing, because it permits us to undergo this intense refinement of our souls without being harmed emotionally in the process.

Even so, most of us hope for at least some semblance of consolation while we are waiting. Often, we receive none. Instead, we enter into a place of desolation, and we wonder if we are being punished for some wrongdoing or why these horrific attacks keep intensifying. As we will explore in subsequent chapters, obscure faith actually increases in us when we don't feel or sense any sort of consolations from God. We move from a place of feeling to a place of knowing.[13]

Fortunately, we do receive refreshment from time to time, even in the desert. God knows our limitations and does not typically expect us to undergo years and years of desolation without any sort of reprieve. We may receive the unexpected consolation in order to rejuvenate our resolve in fidelity towards God in the desert, but then we will certainly anticipate those periods of spiritual aridity when they do return. God often blesses us with some sort of significant sign that does appeal to our feelings and senses shortly before we begin to carry a heavier cross.

How can desolation be our consolation? Quite simply, God is drawn to our misery. Our condition of brokenness and wretchedness actually appeals to His mercy even more than our fervent devotions in times of great joy and celebration. Archbishop Luis M. Martinez described desolation as a "tragic beauty,"[14] which paradoxically means that our crosses indicate our close relationship with God. He *blesses* us with suffering at times, including periods of desert waiting, so that we might know how much He loves us!

The inability to feel, see, or hear God in our daily lives does not indicate a lack of love; on the contrary, it represents His beckoning for us to draw ever nearer to His wounds and Passion, perhaps so that we might come to console Him through our sufferings offered in love. Moments of desolation in our lives are interior clues that God is answering our prayers to become holy, to attain the perfection of eternity: "The ways of God for attaining perfection are ways of struggle, of dryness, of humiliations, and even of falls."[15]

So, you see, our weaknesses in desolation do not repel Him. They draw Him nearer to us, though we don't feel it. God never withdraws His grace from us, only the feelings associated with grace. This is how love is refined in the "crucible of desolation,"[16] so that it may be perfected and pure before we attain our ultimate goal of Heaven.

You and I wrestle with our crosses, most especially when they involve dryness, no emotional response, and desolation. But when we reach the point of either accepting or denying God's will for us to suffer, the choice is to either become transformed through our crosses or to reject *His Cross*. Desolation teaches us that our trials are never for naught. They are not meant to punish us or push us away from God. Instead, they have an incredible ability to sanctify us.

We must believe, as Boethius eloquently once wrote, "Good fortune deceives, but misfortune teaches."[17] Moments of consolation in our lives rarely deepen our faith. They feed it, of course, with sweet, heavenly nectar. Perhaps it is because we are in an infancy of faith that we need this sweetness in order to learn and practice faithfulness. But pain and suffering through the trials of desolation are the real teachers in our spiritual journeys. That is, in part, why desolation is so beneficial to our interior growth.

Obscure faith, or blind faith, is not necessarily clear, but it is always certain. St. Ignatius of Loyola sagaciously suggests that "in times of desolation, there must be no changing."[18] This means that we should remain as faithful to God through prayer and devotion during our times of trial as we are during times of tremendous outpouring of consolations.

As God eclipses our senses, He opens the eyes of our hearts. With hearts made of flesh and not of stone (see Ezekiel 36:26), we are more apt to fix our attention on the path to Heaven. Faith is our beacon, our shining star that illuminates this road, so that all of the peripheral experiences don't matter to us anymore. Our ambition is simply to remain on this road, which is filled with abasements and humiliations, because faith tells us that it will assuredly lead us home to Heaven.

Do we expect to arrive in Heaven without suffering? Or do we truly love God for His own sake, thus desiring to live as He lived, including living His Passion? Though our own experience of passion is, in fact, the ultimate means of concluding our life's calling (which I explain in more depth in Chapter 6), we know that passion leads to resurrection. And our resurrection is Heaven. Perfection isn't about what we do; it's a matter of a sincere and contrite heart.

As Archbishop Luis M. Martinez beautifully articulates, "One arrives at perfection by paths that are strewn with imperfections...God does not ask for the perfection of our conduct, but for the perfection of our heart..."[19]

The perfection of the heart: this is what God wants from us! If it requires us to die a million little deaths or perhaps in one blaze of glory through martyrdom, so be it. If perfection of the heart implies that we must suffer countless trials and agonizing torments that blind our senses through desert waiting, may it be done to us as God sees fit. We know He does not enjoy our pain, but He also knows that love is, ultimately, perfected by it. And that is why, dear friends, we should not fear the desert or desolations. We should instead welcome them with open arms, knowing that God's love for us is so immense that He wishes for us to walk as He walked, to live and die as He did.

May our desert waiting be our gift to Him, then, a gift of consolation that perhaps might assuage the suffering He felt during His Passion.

Chapter Two

Seeking a Hidden God and Resting in Him

*He who made...the world, of His own
freedom, waits upon the world.*

—W. H. Vanstone, *The Stature of Waiting*

Thirty years ago, Sundays were considered to be sacred—a day each week set aside for rest, worship, and family. It never bothered anyone in my family that grocery stores and other retailers were closed, because we planned our weeks around Sundays. Because of this, I always looked forward to the "day of rest" each week, a time I knew would be spent attending Mass, enjoying a leisurely meal with my family, and taking naps.

Today, nearly everything is open 24/7. It was only a few years ago when I noticed the change, and it was jarring. My husband, Ben, and I were driving home from my parents' house, which is a bit of a jog from our rural town, and every city we passed was bustling with activity. We passed strip malls and shopping centers, gas stations and grocery stores, specialty retailers and wineries, ball parks and superstores. Everything was bursting with activity—and it was a Sunday.

Before I sound like a Negative Nelly or fatalist, let me be clear: I'm not opposed to life carrying on with recreation. But Sunday is clearly no longer a day set aside as a day of higher value than the other days of the week, and I find this an incredible misfortune. Sure, some places must remain open on Sundays, such as hospitals, fire stations, and pharmacies, but must everything else be humming with the drone of distraction and busyness?

It seems to me that the switch from Sundays as sacred to "just another day of the week" happened somewhere in the shift of our hectic lives. I'm sure many factors have contributed to extracurricular school activities being scheduled on Sundays, as well as why retailers are open. But, irrespective of other lesser, extraneous variables, it seems that Sundays have fallen off of the calendar as our days of rest because of our godless society. The bottom line is we, as a culture, don't acknowledge God's laws above man's laws. So we have created a system that seems to work more for us than it does for God. Again, what a tragedy.

In order for us to comprehend more fully the reason why rest is of such great importance and how it ties in to our waiting experiences, we must first visit the creation story in Genesis.

CREATION: GOD RESTED

Not long ago, I began homeschooling our oldest daughter, Felicity, for kindergarten. I was duly impressed with her religion book, which followed the liturgical calendar and made the change of seasons and time more enjoyable for her. What was most beneficial, however, was that everything started at the beginning of creation. It was as if we were starting anew with a fresh reminder of how it all began with the breath and word of God our Father.

We lingered over each day of creation, discussing the wonders of nature around us and how God made space, time, and habitat before He filled it with His most prized creation—humanity. Felicity asked questions about the sun, moon, and stars and how light and darkness came to be. We shared our favorite colors found in nature's flowers and the beautiful songbirds we are privileged to hear serenade us in the spring. But what struck me as most notable, though it was not stated as surpassing the rest of creation in any way through the Genesis account, was that *God rested on the seventh day.*

God rested. I pondered that for a bit before delving into an explanation to a six-year-old. Even to my thirty-something brain, it was a wondrous thought—that God, the Alpha and the Omega, the One who has always existed and is our First Source—He Himself *rested*. Why? He certainly didn't need rest. I've always viewed rest as a necessity for us finite creatures, because our bodies cannot carry on with life without breaks from activity. But God! God can do all things. He surpasses the limitations of His creations. He is unfathomable in His infinity. Why would He *choose* to rest?

Quite simply, the answer is that He wanted to teach us about the value of quiet time and periodic hiatuses from our work. And He established that importance when He rested on the seventh day of creation—after all of His work was completed. It's interesting that "keeping holy the Sabbath" then became the third commandment. God specifically instructed us through Moses to work for six days, but to *do no work on the seventh day* (see Exodus 20:8).

Let's dissect this incredibly poignant point from St. Thomas Aquinas about why God rested and the lesson it teaches us: "As God, who made all things, did not rest *in* those things…but rested *in* himself *from* the created works…so we too should learn not to regard the works as the goal, but to rest *from* the works in God himself…"[20] We are not a people of incessant toil. Keeping the Sabbath holy means we don't momentarily put aside our work, yet constantly ruminate over what tasks need to be completed on our to-do lists.

Rather, we rest *from* our work and instead rest *in* God. Resting in God requires the surrender from busyness that we briefly defined in Chapter 1. It means we quiet both our bodies and our minds to a place of solitude, so that we can more fully enter that condition of leisure, or active waiting, in which we attentively listen to God speak to us—be it in the hushed whispers or the brilliant thunder. That is how we move into deeper communion with God, through contemplation and heartfelt communication. Sundays provide an opportunity for us to regularly enter into this communion with God.

Considering that we have regressed from a people who valued balance through appropriate leisure to a people of constant frenzied activity, we would do well to return to the gift we are given in the Sabbath day—the day of rest. It is a day we must set aside all unnecessary work (of course, such things as making meals to feed our families or changing diapers for babies is considered necessary and must be done, regardless of the day of the week). To do so means we are not only following God's commandment but also following what He Himself did after His work of creation was complete.

Who are we to think we do not need to rest? Rest offers our minds and bodies the opportunity for restoration and rejuvenation so that we can continue the work God has given us to complete. Furthermore, waiting often accompanies times of rest and respite. Even if our waiting is regimented on Sundays only, we encounter that desert experience of slow movement, solitude, and quiet. So we can *choose* to rest and wait, just as God chose to rest after creation.

What about the times when God seems to be still within us? Certainly all of us can recall a time or times when we felt that God was not stirring in us as He once did, perhaps when our faith was young and we were zealous to do great things for God. It is true that the Holy Spirit moves in and through and around us at times, but we must also consider the moments when He is still and does not move. We shouldn't assume that His quietude indicates a lack of care or provision for us. In fact, many spiritual writers have contemplated this concept of God "resting in us" and have realized that it means He is closer to us than ever before. Let's ponder some of these points.

The stillness of waiting is often agonizing, as we discussed in Chapter 1. It's often more so when we believe God has abandoned us due to His lack of movement or even lack of response to our prayers. When we do not feel His presence or hear His voice, our inclination is to believe He has left us altogether, that we have somehow been forsaken—perhaps due to punishment or otherwise. But our God is certainly one of paradoxes, and it seems He operates in this way because He longs for us to chase Him, to seek Him. There is evidence of this enough in Scripture, and we will visit some of these verses to elaborate the point.

GOD WAITS FOR US

God waits for us. He does this by hiding Himself at times—not always, but at times—so that we may seek Him. In his classic, *Worshipping A Hidden God*, Archbishop Luis M. Martinez beautifully writes, "A hidden God must be sought…He is present everywhere, but everywhere He is concealed."[21] He bases this thought on the verse from Isaiah 45:15, which states, "Truly with you God is hidden." What does this mean exactly? Well, as we have recalled, God is present to us through all of His creation—every detail, every flower, every color and form of vegetation or animal life.

Quite possibly, God waits in the abyss of our souls so that we can discover Him through self-abasement. Humility is the key to finding God, and waiting often increases humility in us. Why is this so? Because we do not see immediate results. We do not see what God is doing beneath the surface, deep in the recesses and crevices of our being—where it is so dark that perhaps we do not know that particular aspect of ourselves. As we grow in humility, we grow in self-knowledge. We are then able to see the darkness within us—both holy (where God waits for us) and unholy (our sins)—and lower ourselves so that He may lift us up. It is through humility that we fulfill the Scripture, "He must increase, but I must decrease" (John 3:30).

Yet there are times when we do not see, feel, or hear Him, though He is everywhere around and within us. He chooses to hide Himself—to ask us to wait to hear, see, or feel His presence again—so that we may seek Him. To the one who loves, seeking the lover is never an impediment to love, never an imposition. It's always a delight to seek one's beloved, to wait for Him to reveal Himself once again.

Song of Songs, the beautiful romance between God as lover and us, His beloved, opens with this lamentation of longing: "On my bed at night I sought him whom my soul loves – I sought him but I did not find him…Let me seek him whom my soul loves" (1:1-2). So, you see, there are times in our lives when God wishes that we wait upon Him through the pining of love. If our entire love story with God only involved that which He gave us through consolations, signs, and all sorts of spiritual ecstasies, of what true value would our love for Him be?

It is only when we give something that hurts—often through the longing that waiting brings—that our love becomes refined, more deeply arduous, truly authentic, and pure. When He is still, do not fear the seeming absence from your soul. Enter into that abyss where you may find Him sleeping, and seek Him more ardently and desperately. Do not cease until you have found "him whom your soul loves," so that you may hold him and "not let him go" (see Song of Songs 1:5a).

There will be times still when you believe your searching is done in vain. During those times, I encourage you to ponder a few additional thoughts on the beauty of a God who waits for us through rest and stillness.

Let us visit the book of Isaiah and contemplate these words: "For my thoughts are not your thoughts, nor are your ways my ways, says the Lord" (55:8). Waiting for God to reveal Himself to us often feels lonely, desolate, and excruciating, but He may choose to communicate with us in clandestine ways. The Eucharist is one way He conceals Himself—in that small, thin wafer that does not speak, yet beckons us with a constancy that only love understands. God operates in this hidden way because He far surpasses our limited scope of understanding and viewing the world around us or even ourselves. We cannot fully grasp every reason God chooses to move in us or wait in stillness. And this requires trust.

Archbishop Luis M. Martinez also encourages us: "How often, when we think that we are most distant from God, we are most closely united to Him!"[22] During those periods of your life when all is quiet and appears to be lost, when God has concealed Himself from you in one form or fashion, be uplifted by the assurance that He cannot be seen or heard or felt, because He abides more deeply and securely in your heart.

Many stories involving Jesus's life also reveal the beauty of waiting for a hidden God. We can look to the first Christmas as St. Joseph and the Blessed Mother sought shelter in Bethlehem for the Son of God to be born. Let us imagine that St. Joseph's desperation increases as he pounds from door to door, begging to find lodging. He may have felt that his efforts were fruitless, that with each knock, it was a vain attempt that only led to disappointment. We, too, feel this way as we knock on the doors of opportunity, only to be met with silence or rejection. Waiting can grant us no response after no response, and we feel that our efforts are futile.

But, as Richard Frederick Clarke, S.J. wrote, "God prepares His saints and chosen ones for some signal blessing. We must not be cast down by the fruitlessness of our efforts. It is a sign that some great grace is close at hand."[23] Could it be, then, that waiting for agonizing lengths of time, even waiting fruitlessly, is actually concealing a greater blessing for us? Yes, it is true, and we must cling to this hope as we wait for God to be revealed to us once again.

Meanwhile, the Blessed Mother likely prayed in silent patience as her spouse sought shelter for her and the soon-to-be newborn Christ-Child. Since she always "pondered these things in her heart" (see Luke 2:19), she resigned herself to whatever was God's will, though it might not have been as she or St. Joseph had hoped or planned. She knew, from the instant of the Annunciation, that suffering would accompany this incredible task of bearing God's Son, but she trusted God with such confidence as she waited for what would happen next. Here, Richard Frederick Clarke reflects, "Blessed are those who wait patiently in such a spirit. God will soon fulfill all the desires of their heart."[24]

There are countless scenarios in our own lives in which we'd prefer to take charge and control the outcome of a potential hardship. If we were waiting as St. Joseph and Our Lady waited in Bethlehem, would we remain patient as God's will unfolded before us, or would we, out of fear and impending hopelessness, try to manage the situation ourselves? During those times in our life when we are waiting as St. Joseph and Mary waited, when we are desperate for answers and none arrive with immediacy, let us do as they did and expect that great things are on the horizon for us if we remain where we are, faithful to God and waiting on His response.

Revelation After a Time of Concealment

From the cradle to the grave, Jesus's life exemplifies the gift of waiting for Him to reveal Himself after a time of concealment. Holy Saturday is a stark reminder to me of waiting in the midst of darkness, when all seems lost and we must wait with hope for the fulfillment of His promise that He will rise again. The three days when Jesus was in the tomb was a time of overwhelming waiting for the Apostles. As each day passed, doubt crept in. It is the same for us—the longer we must wait, the harder it becomes. But tomb waiting—the stillness of darkness when God conceals Himself from us for a time—is much like desert waiting in what it can teach us.

As Father Peter Cameron says, "Like the holy women who kept watch at Jesus' tomb, we wait in hope in the darkness of this night. And if, with them, some doubt still lingers in our hearts – 'Who will roll away the stone?' – we know that patience and persistence will soon give us the assurance that we seek. Christ's new life rolls away every stone, every obstacle, every stumbling-block in our souls. He calls us to keep vigil so that we may avail ourselves to his saving grace.

"If in our silence and solitude we feel lonely and lost, the Mother of God comes in search of us...We wait in stillness, enfolded in Mary's eternal love, devoted to being about the Father's business."[25] Our Lady is, indeed, our oasis when we do not feel close to her Son. She refreshes us with her presence of mercy and lures us closer to Him through her own sorrowful heart. Her waiting is our waiting.

What holy assurance we have in our waiting! Every aspect of our lives—the silence, the moments of respite, the holy darkness, when we are alone or lonely, when we are afraid, our desert experience and tomb waiting—carries a grain of promise that must swiftly and softly lead us away from doubt and fear and toward the God who never fails us, the God of the Resurrection.

When the Resurrection does arrive—as it most certainly does—it is by way of what St. John of the Cross calls "obscure faith."[26] Obscure faith leads us to the God whom we seek, who may be sleeping in our hearts, in the tomb, or in the boat with the Apostles. Only by way of obscure faith, which is not by way of sight or any "sensible pleasure,"[27] but through belief in God's goodness alone, can we discover Him whom we seek. Then He will reveal Himself once more in our lives, and the waiting—for a time—will be over. Let us rejoice in the resurrections that await us!

Finally, we must not become disturbed when God chooses to sleep and remain still for a time in our lives. Our doubt only signifies our lack of obscure faith. We mustn't wonder why God seems absent. Instead, we should thank Him for such a gift as waiting can be, because we know it is a call to a deeper, more ardent and authentic faith that isn't satisfied with what our senses perceive alone. In time, Jesus will come. He will hasten to bring us the desires of our heart. We must only remain faithful to the Church, to prayer, and to doing all in the midst of our desert experience with joy and earnest expectation.

We will conclude with this word of encouragement from Father Cameron: "Do we expect enough from God? Does his hiddenness intimidate us and stir us up? Christ will come without delay. To meet him with joy we need only devote ourselves to the teachings of the Church. For that sacred doctrine fills us with the steadfastness we need to give ourselves wholly to God, to wait for his appearance at the wedding feast, and to respond to his miraculous power when we feel let down and forgotten."[28]

Chapter Three

Hidden Opportunities in Times of Waiting

*Since the mysteries of God are always living
and active now, a real birth of the Word will
occur in our souls. The Author of grace will
come to reign within us more profoundly and
more fully, and consequently he will reach
others more effectively through us.*

— Mother Marie Des Douleurs,
"Meditation of the Day:
Our Glorious Heritage," *Magnificat*

I'm looking outside my bedroom window and notice that the world seems to wait—for what is unclear, but the fact is that all is still these winter months as the holiday rush dies down and comes to an end. Nature, in its winter sleep, seems to communicate death. Even when I walk my dog on our daily route, all appears to be lost. There are no signs of any life as we pass endless deciduous trees, seeing the frozen earth blanketed in snow and ice, and hearing not even distant echoes of beloved songbirds.

The conifers and occasional romping squirrel, though, do remind me that life does, in fact, exist in the harshest and coldest of winter days and nights. Life does continue, albeit in a sort of holding pattern. The flowering trees may be at rest the next few months, but in the spring they will burst forth with their fragrant and lovely blooms. And life will be evident and vibrant once again.

Active and Passive Waiting

The great spiritual writers spoke about two types of waiting, both active and passive. Nature provides us with its wisdom, because God speaks to us through His creation. Active waiting involves expectancy and vigilance, much like we see in the Visitation of Mary to her cousin, Elizabeth. The evergreen trees that do not die and the fur-bearing critters that do not disappear in the winter remind me of active waiting. They continue to seek until they find what they are searching for, and they do not waver even as the rest of the world slips into a quiet coma. We will delve more deeply into the spirituality of active waiting in Chapter 5.

Passive waiting, which will be discussed extensively in Chapter 6, accounts for most of what we tend to consider "a waste of time." Much of our waiting includes what is done to us rather than what we seek out on our own. We can remain watchful during times of passive waiting, but the main aspect of waiting for what will be done to us involves our own *passion*, or suffering as Jesus did. (This is why an entire chapter must be devoted to unraveling the profundity of passive waiting.) The majority of nature reflects this type of waiting, such as when the maple leaves fall off the branches in late autumn and crumble underfoot in early winter. There is a sort of self-annihilation that must occur during times of passive waiting.

But let us never forget that waiting produces the fruit of endurance through resurrection. We await—whether actively or passively—the unfurling of our own fresh sprigs of green and clean, delicate blossoms of interior resurrection as winter gives way to spring in our lives.

Waiting Is Not Wasting

As I was reading more about this phenomenon of spiritual waiting, it occurred to me that waiting is not wasting. I think most of us believe the contrary, which is why it befits us to set the foundation of how purposeful and intentional waiting *always* is in our lives. Consider the wisdom from the saints, all of whom believed that everything is grace and we should thank God for all that happens to us, whether good or ill. When we accept all that happens to us, including periods of our lives when we wait, our love for God becomes stronger and more purified. We grow in virtue.

St. Catherine of Siena, the eloquent Dominican Doctor of the Church, explains it this way:

> Now, since the Son has given his life for us with such blazing love, we ought to be convinced that every burden that is laid on us, *whether agreeable or disagreeable*, from whatever source it may come, is given us out of love and not out of hatred; it is given only for our good, so that we may achieve the end for which we were created. And we should realize that our burdens are no greater or smaller than time – and our time is as small as the point of a needle. In breadth and in length they are nothing at all. So our burdens are tiny, finite.[29]

So, you see, waiting, though considered a terrible burden at times, is really for the greater good of our souls. If we consider the agony of how long we must wait in terms of just a flicker on the map of eternity, perhaps waiting will not be such an onus to us. I think of how St. Monica waited thirty years before her son, St. Augustine, was converted from his perverse and debaucherous lifestyle. Hers was both a passive and an active waiting,[30] though she entered into that time with confidence in God's holy will for the good of her son.

Let's define more clearly the difference between active and passive waiting before moving forward with how waiting hides a particular grace within it for our good. Active waiting is when we are the subject of what happens. For instance, if I say, "Jesus brought with Him Peter, James, and John to the mountain," then Jesus is the subject. He is actively *doing* something. Active waiting implies community.

Passive waiting, however, is when we move from being the subject to the object. In this circumstance, we would say, "Peter, James, and John went with Jesus to the mountain." In that sentence, which essentially communicates the same message as the first, Jesus becomes the *object*, rather than the subject. And when we become the object, we are handed over to others or to circumstance. We do not control what happens to us or what the outcome of a particular situation is. This is *passion*, because we are entirely awaiting what others will do to us.

As we have already said, passive waiting accounts for most of our waiting experiences—what happens to us rather than what we enter into actively. *Passive waiting is our passion*. When God permits us to enter into this type of waiting—when we become objects rather than subjects of our lives—we receive an invitation to journey with Jesus from Gethsemane to Golgotha. Some examples of passive waiting include when we are in a long line at the store, waiting on hold for a customer service representative, wondering when our neighbor will return our lawnmower, and being stuck in a traffic jam.

There are a plethora of examples we could conjure about passive waiting. Since it accounts for most of what we experience, it's important for us to learn how we can transform our reaction to waiting from impatience or anger to surrender and prayer. We can make passive waiting spiritually transformative through sacrifices, acts of mortification, offering up the situation, etc. While waiting in that line, smile at the cashier and offer a compliment. When stuck in that traffic jam, pray a Rosary.

Active waiting, however, is much like Advent waiting. We enter into this type of waiting by our own accord, of our own choosing. We expect something to happen when we wait with vigilance, with earnest hope. Often, active waiting leads us to a deeper sense of community, which means that we desire to wait with another person rather than alone. A beautiful example of this type of waiting occurred during Mary's visit to her cousin, Elizabeth, while they were both pregnant.

We learn that as soon as Our Lady received word from St. Gabriel about Elizabeth being pregnant "even in her old age" (see Luke 1:36), she went "in haste" to visit Elizabeth. Isn't that interesting? She immediately went to spend time with Elizabeth, and why was that? Some may speculate that she was trying to evade the judgment of her peers and family in Nazareth, but in reality, it was because she had just received a promise—to become the Mother of God—and a message of hope wrapped in that promise—that Elizabeth would also bear a child!

When we wait in joyful anticipation, we remember that "nothing will be impossible for God." Like both Mary and St. Elizabeth, we carry the seed of God's promise within us. We are pregnant with expectation, but that seed must germinate for a time before the promise is fully realized.

Once the Blessed Mother reached her cousin's home, Elizabeth greeted her with the beloved words we hear each Advent: "Blessed is she who believed that the promise made her by the Lord would be fulfilled" (see Luke 1:45). By waiting for a time in community with each other, both Mary and Elizabeth affirmed each other in their expectant joy. They encouraged each other "that something was happening that was worth waiting for."[31]

Another perspective, or definition, of active waiting could be the philosophical term "leisure." In his modern classic on the marvel and wonder of philosophy, Josef Pieper explains that "leisure implies...an attitude of non-activity, of inward calm, of silence; it means not being 'busy' but letting things happen."[32] There is receptivity in this active, or Advent, waiting. It's not an empty void or lack of noise; it's attentive listening and anticipating God's response.

Entering into active waiting isn't nearly as cumbersome as the passion of passive waiting, is it? Somehow the joy of waiting for a promise to be fulfilled seems exciting and even adventurous. And when we wait with others in that eager hope, it's not nearly as desolating as when we are in the desert experience alone. But for Our Lady and St. Elizabeth, waiting was not something to muddle through. Their time was precious, and it was exponentially more so because of their time spent together: "Waiting together, nurturing what has already begun, expecting its fulfillment – that is the meaning of marriage, friendship, community, and the Christian life."[33]

Even when Jesus entered His own Passion in the Garden of Gethsemane, He longed for community in His own waiting experience. Recall how He asked the Apostles to keep watch with Him, to stay awake. He also asks us to stay awake with Him, whether we are entering a period of activity or resting, active or passive waiting: "Jesus had asked them to watch with him so that they might share fully in the mystery of the moment: Jesus makes a total gift of himself to the will of the Father."[34]

Waiting is much like that for us, too. God wants us to participate, so as to share, in the Paschal Mystery, so that we might come to receive and accept His total gift of self, thus going forth to offer Him our entire lives as a gift to Him. Only through waiting do we come to understand the value of this mystery. So let us wait with Him and for Him.

As we grow in our interior lives, we learn that nearly all of it involves some sort of waiting. Because God does not operate according to our timelines and deadlines, we must learn to enjoy or offer up the times when we await His movement in and through us. Something that can aid us on this journey is to recall the times in which God's promises have come to fruition after months or years of waiting for something more to happen in our lives.

Pregnancy is one of those perfect examples of active waiting, which is why the Visitation is so appropriate in illustrating the point of waiting as joyful, hope-filled expectation. When I was pregnant with our first child, I remember well the months of waiting, for two reasons. One, it took me a while to get pregnant after a painful bout of infertility. So, discovering this new life within me was unbearably exciting! Two, waiting for the child you have long prayed for and desired to welcome into your heart and home is difficult—unless you are entering into that time actively, through prayers of praise and gratitude.

We all know that we are called to something greater than stagnancy and mediocrity in our lives, yet we do not all receive a clear indication of what that call might be. And that, too, makes waiting all the more difficult for us. But when we wait actively, we share our joy and we are certain that God will bring about the longing of our heart's desire, so that what was promised will most assuredly be fulfilled.

In order to fully enter into active waiting with the same joy as Mary and Elizabeth experienced, we need to cling to the promise that what God has begun in our lives will not return to Him void (see Isaiah 55:11) but will indeed come about in a most glorious and splendorous way: "The secret of waiting is the faith that the seed has been planted, that something has begun. Active waiting means to be present fully to the moment, in the conviction that something is happening where you are and that you want to be present to it. A waiting person is someone who is present to the moment, who believes that this moment is 'the moment.'"[35]

EXPECTANT FAITH

When we begin to understand and appreciate both active and passive waiting through the lens of gratitude, everything changes—everything. Life somehow becomes renewed in every aspect, and we awaken to the possibilities to which we were previously blinded. If we also consider active waiting to be a form of leisure, we learn that there is a type of surrender that occurs when one is receptive to marveling at who God is and what He made. Fr. Solanus Casey beautifully merged the understanding and need for us to surrender to God's will while also retaining a heroic confidence in His providence.

Several years ago, I was introduced to this saint-in-the-making, Blessed Fr. Solanus Casey, O.F.M. Cap., whose simple spirituality intrigued me. One of his most famous maxims was, "Thank God ahead of time." The simplicity of his spirituality included this concept, which he defined as "expectant faith."

When we thank God ahead of time, we are not presumptuously assuming that He will give us everything we want. Instead, we are thanking God for whatever He sees fit to happen to us—that passive waiting—whatever it takes to draw us nearer to Him and assist us toward our heavenly goal. There is a particular level of confidence when we pray in this way, thanking God for both the good and the struggles that are sure to ensue. Our faith becomes more secure. We move from a faith that relies on consolations to the obscure faith of which St. John of the Cross explained.

Expectant faith, then, is what Our Lady and St. Elizabeth demonstrated in their relationship with each other. They knew God was doing great things, not only to them, but for the entire world! What if we believed the same in our own day and age, so hungry for hope? What if we truly expected God to do wondrous things in our lives, thanking Him for all that was necessary for us to endure in order to reach the vision He has in mind for us!

Father Solanus knew well that in order for faith to be rooted in good soil (see Matthew 13), it must be fostered through the practice of gratitude. Father Donald Haggerty elaborates this point on how gratitude moves us to a deeper awareness of the good in our lives:

> A prayer of gratitude will always influence our perceptions outside of prayer. Once we are in the habit of thanking God for *all* that is happening in our life, including the harder challenges, a new realization awakens. The providential nature of events begins to show itself more. We 'see' the hand of God more at work or at least trust implicitly that his reasons will show themselves in time.[36]

This is what Father Solanus meant by expectant faith: that pregnant, active waiting with a sense of gratitude for all that God gives us or allows to befall us. Waiting with confidence in God means that we know He will never fail us. The waiting will eventually give way to new life, a new birth, and we will then express more deeply our love by sharing with others what God has done for us.

From Community to Contemplation

We've established that active waiting leads us to community, or neighborliness. We become more acutely aware of others' needs, as well as our own, when we enter into this type of vigilant expectancy. What we have not yet explained is that active waiting often *precedes* passive waiting.

God desires that we enter into community before we can pass into contemplation. Contemplation is the fruit of passive waiting, in which we transition from activity to ponderous solitude. Living with others is a necessary prerequisite for contemplation, because our relationship with others exposes our sins and weaknesses.

Let's suppose that I feel *drawn* toward asceticism, that I'd prefer to become a hermit and spend my life studying Scripture, philosophizing, and perhaps writing. But I am called to the married life, not a religious vocation. How could an eremitical lifestyle overlap with a vocation to marriage and family?

Both could very well be separate aspects of my life, but only in relation to my *interior life*. Contemplation—e.g., the lure to solitude and reflecting deeply and meaningfully—is subsequent to community—e.g., living with and among others (like my husband and children). So it's not a literal shift from living as a wife and mother to becoming a recluse; it's a spiritual one.

After I first enter into an *active* relationship with others, then I may be drawn away from constant communication and interaction—into a more contemplative interior desert so to speak. Living in community is a prerequisite to contemplation, because the constant and close interaction with people reflects in me my tendency toward selfishness or my negative attitudes about the division of responsibility in the home. Sharing a dwelling space with others also mirrors back to me my weakness toward irascibility and irritability.

One might wonder how this works for the rare person who is called to live as a hermit. Is it possible to achieve contemplation without the prerequisite of communal formation, or is this a ubiquitous relationship? The short answer is that, yes, it is possible for a person to reach the state of contemplation without direct or constant access to a community of other people. I would argue, however, that this is rare.

To understand this more deeply, it's important to distinguish between acquired and infused contemplation. Both, of course, require access to the intellect, the use of which is not necessarily contingent upon conversing or relating with others. *However, God created us to be a people of relationship.* Therefore, a person authentically called to live as a consecrated hermit or even anchoress would be a rare exception to the need for a cycle of both community and contemplation.

Acquired contemplation is the "fruit of our own efforts."[37] This means that anyone has the potential to reach this type of contemplation. We might be drawn toward studying Scripture or theology or doctrines of the Faith, etc. We yearn to grow in knowledge of God in order to understand Him more fully or to enter into a deeper relationship with Him. In this way, knowledge by way of the intellect—which is initiated by an act of the will—paves the way for contemplation. This, of course, can be done without engaging in ongoing conversations with others or learning from a human relationship.

Infused contemplation, in contrast, is strictly initiated by God's efforts upon our souls.[38] This is a more mystical form of prayer in which the Holy Spirit moves us through both active and passive states of union with Him. It is impossible for a person to initiate infused contemplation. It is a pure gift of God to souls who have spiritually advanced to the point where the soul is completely receptive to the promptings of the Holy Spirit. Again, this type of contemplation is entirely segregated from human relationships.

Let's go back, however, to the consecrated hermit or anchoress, two vocations which were much more common in the early days of Christianity, yet which still exist today. The hermit or anchoress was still birthed by a woman and, we'll assume, raised by someone—a family, a community of religious sisters or monks, etc. The point is that at some time during their formative years, they interacted with other people, likely their parents, siblings, cousins, etc. I cannot think of a single instance in which an adult who eventually lives a life of solitude given to God has never learned the value and beauty of encountering other people through relationship.

So, even for those who live a solitary life of sanctity and constant prayer, the Lord likely heavily pruned their ability toward contemplation in their younger years when they were still growing in self-knowledge by way of living in and amongst a community of people who reflected back to them their weaknesses or tried their patience in some form. The vast majority of us, then, probably move between communal formation and contemplation several times throughout our lives, based on God's lead.

Active waiting invites me to reflect upon my sinful patterns of behavior and grow in virtue by the opportunities presented to me when I encounter others in my life through relationship. This perfection in virtue always segues into contemplation as I spiritually mature. The desert periodically beckons us away from living in community and into a phase of life in which contemplation is more suitable.[39]

Another example is that sometimes we belong to a group or community (e.g., a Bible study) that fuels our faith. We become stronger and better together and so are more equipped to enter the mission field of life after drawing upon the support we receive from our faith community.

Community, as we have stated, always prepares us for the desert of contemplation. The twelve Apostles followed Jesus together, but they also forged an irrevocable brotherhood with each other, a bond of community. All those years they were apprenticed, everything that Jesus drew out of them—their gifts and sins and deepest thoughts—were to eventually lead them away from each other and into the world.

It is in the scattering that we often lose ourselves or at least feel lost for a time. We, like the Twelve, have found security and assurance in our community circles. We don't want to be moved or shifted away from the foundation and into an unknown place that offers us no guarantees.

But without this commissioning, we would not have the universal Church. If the Apostles had remained together in the Holy Land, who would have evangelized the rest of the world? They needed to believe that their time together was a preparation, a test of greater things to come.

No one who is called to do great things ever believes he is fully prepared for the task he is called to do. Doubts are inevitable. But for the one who has been divinely apprenticed, the commissioning is worth the risk of failure and uncertainty. This is because he lives in Christ. Jesus Himself has formed his soul, refined it and purged it. It is the Holy Spirit, then, who lives and breathes and operates in him.

"It is no longer I, but Christ who lives in me" (see Galatians 2:20). The disciple who has been called away must leave, not cleave to what he already knows. He must venture into unknown territory, believing that what is impossible for him to accomplish is possible for God to accomplish *through* him.

The Apostles, by virtue of their bond, must have felt torn as they parted ways after Pentecost. They must have shared a deep, lingering sorrow over their time together coming to an end, despite the joy of knowing the Holy Spirit had infused them with God Himself.

Even so, before Jesus ascended into Heaven, He told them that greater things were to come. Did the Apostles question this as we often do? Their Savior had just left them, mere humans, to continue His divine work! They had His Presence in the Eucharist, yes. They would be given the Holy Spirit, yes. But they no longer had Jesus walking on earth with them. How could greater things happen without Jesus with them, walking at their sides?

As we are sent forth from community into our own desert experiences, we might feel the same. We might wonder how and when God will use us to bring about something greater and more beautiful than what we've shared in our circles of friendship and fellowship.

We will likely feel ill-equipped. Spiritually speaking, our sins and weaknesses are so evident to us that we cannot imagine being useful to God! But this is why humility is so necessary. Humility acknowledges the weakness, yet clings to God's mercy. Humility would have us know, without doubt, that all things are possible with God.

So we must leave our communities when Jesus calls us elsewhere, even and especially when we don't know where He's leading us. The desert of contemplation bears fruit in its own time.

Remember how we said in Chapter 1 that we might experience the desert moments in our lives—moments when we do not feel any sensible pleasures from our devotions or prayers? We do not see, hear, or feel God's presence. In a sense, the desert symbolizes a rather arid and desolate time of life, which opposes our concupiscent nature that seeks pleasure and comfort.

Wandering in the wilderness, as we discussed, has a definite and fruitful purpose in our lives, should we acquiesce to God's plan for us while we are there. It is through the periodic desert living that we become less aware of our lack and more keenly aware of God—who He is—fearing Him with a wider love that somehow expands through the desolations and trials we undergo.

This is why active waiting is such an important transition into the more arduous passive waiting of the desert. We must first understand who we are in relation to others and amend our sinful patterns before entering the bitterness of desert living. Most of us will not live most or all of our earthly lives in a state of acquired contemplation,[40] but we may very well experience specific moments or longer periods of time when God calls us away from community and into a deeper communication with Him.

When we seek our Lover with our whole heart and soul, we will likely find ourselves longing to know more and more about how to love God as we ought. Prayer leads us to contemplation, but it is not sufficient for such depth of communication with the Divine. We ought to always "pray without ceasing" (see 1 Thessalonians 5:16), but prayer alone will not carry us to the heights of contemplative love.

Contemplation is the aspect of our interior lives that bridges the gap between our earthly and eternal existence. It is the one method of union with God that we may taste here on Earth but will everlastingly know in Heaven. This is because contemplation goes beyond reciting prayers, even beautiful spontaneous prayers. Contemplation is the commencement of our search for God through active waiting. Through it, we attain communion with our Lover in such a way that no words are necessary.

So, dear souls, you see now that waiting leads to love. And love is so much more than what we feel or experience. It transcends our existential understanding of virtue based on our senses or even our intellect. Pure love, attained by way of the journey of passive waiting, draws us to a fusion of what cannot be described adequately in words with our Lover. He waits for us, and we allow Him to wait. We wait for Him, and He will not delay in meeting us in the most intimate recesses of our longings, which are to never be separated from Him.

CHAPTER FOUR

FROM WORKING TO WAITING— ACHIEVING OR RECEIVING?

I wonder as I wander out under the sky
How Jesus the Saviour did come for to die
For poor on'ry people like you and like I;
I wonder as I wander out under the sky.

— John Jacob Niles, "I Wonder as I Wander"

As a child, I learned the value and importance of work from my parents. Both were very diligent in the tasks they set their minds to, my father in providing for our family financially and my mother through her care for the hearth and home. Education was also emphasized as work, so I put my nose to the grindstone early on and set my ambitions high. In school, I became known as the overachieving, straight-A student by my peers, which I took as a compliment. But, once failure arrived (as it inevitably does), I was crushed beyond measure. It didn't make sense for me to be rejected for jobs after college when I'd worked so relentlessly my entire life.

Work, of course, is good. There are several Scripture passages that discuss the importance of toiling for our food and the rewards of the laborer. But what happens when we place our entire identities into what we achieve? For some, it may mean that achievement always comes naturally and steadily. Many will accomplish all they've set to acquire in life: financial security, a cushy job (or at least one they enjoy), luxury cars and newly-built homes. Many of us set out to achieve our version of the "American Dream," though most of us will become sorely disappointed when our dreams turn to dust.

Not all work, however, is beneficial, as we covered in Chapter 2. We mentioned that the early pagan philosophers opined that toil and labor was man's highest good to achieve in life, but Thomas Aquinas clarified this point from a Christian worldview: "Not all work is difficult, and not everything that is difficult is meritorious."[41] Work, without any concept of value or virtue, is essentially barren and meaningless. That is why it behooves us to visit the notion of something we all face in life: moving from a place of activity to resting, or waiting.

There often comes a time in our lives when we move from working to waiting, which means we move from that active state of doing to a more passive state of being. And, for many of us, this is the most difficult aspect of living. We may lose our independence as we age. Perhaps we become incapacitated for a time following a surgery or accident. Some of us are thrust into the world of caregiving for a disabled child, who is entirely dependent upon us for care.

And when this state of helplessness befalls us, we tend to bemoan it, don't we? We writhe and grumble when we are cared for—either that, or we guiltily apologize that we have become such a "burden" to the ones caring for us. In our modern day, autonomy is the highest goal for which we should strive, and when we are unable to care for ourselves, even temporarily, somehow we feel ashamed of our state in life. It's as if the helpless person isn't worth as much as the independent one.

Helplessness is a condition in which we receive, without effort on our part, the gift of community through other people's works of mercy. We are the recipient of their holy efforts, which means we can choose to receive beauty, goodness, and virtue from them during our period of dependence. As we move from activity to receptivity, we are given an opportunity to see that the gift of what others do to and for us is as much, if not *more*, satisfying than what results from our hard work.

"During times of waiting, our status changes from 'working' to 'waiting,' from the role of subject to object, from 'doing' to 'being done to,'"[42] expounds W. H. Vanstone. Our response to becoming the object (passive waiting) rather than the subject of our lives (active waiting) can include several spiritual obstacles that either mold us into more resilient people or cause us to crumble in a heap. When we move from working to waiting, we likely will encounter the temptations of fear, discouragement, and doubt while we wander in the desert.

Even if we remain faithful to the Lord's call in our lives, we will likely experience missional loneliness and holy tension while we wait for His promise to be fulfilled in us. We can either respond rashly and impulsively, or we can allow our passion to shape every aspect of ourselves so that our identity becomes solidly grounded in *who we are* rather than in *what we do*.

So, while we wait, our life "must depend not so much on what [we] achieve as on what [we] receive."[43] And this dependency, more often than not, really stings our pride. We may not freely admit this, but we may not only think less of ourselves when we are in a state of receiving help from another person, but we may also think others are inferior when they are disabled, cognitively impaired, living in a group home, or under the care of hospice.

Theologically, most of us realize that every human life carries equal value and dignity. No one person or type of person is worth more than another. But when we are faced with our own helpless condition or someone else's, we confront a stark reality that we cannot control everything that happens to us or even most of what we experience. Despite an intellectual "knowing" that helplessness does not equate to inferiority, we may feel some sense of sorrow or loss:

> Sometimes we wait with dread for the onset or occurrence of something which…we know to be necessary or appropriate or even beneficial to ourselves…We dread the imminent onset of strain or danger or pain, but we know with our rational faculties that what lies ahead is 'for the best.'[44]

Is the suffering of waiting really "for the best"? In this chapter, let's explore what happens when we move from a condition of working to waiting—from potential spiritual pitfalls to the illumination and discovery of mission.

"DO NOT LET YOUR HEARTS BE TROUBLED OR AFRAID."

Jesus consoled His Apostles with these words, spoken at the Last Supper. He Himself had moved from a place of active ministry to being "handed over" to His Passion. He permitted the Father's will to be done to Him, despite the very human temptation toward discouragement and fear. As Henri Nouwen elucidates, "The more afraid we are, the harder waiting becomes."[45]

We all cringe when any sort of physical, emotional, or spiritual pain strikes. What typical person would enjoy suffering? Even the saints who moved from accepting their cross to welcoming it took time to truly desire to suffer for the sake of love. In Jesus's words, we remember that He is always with us and that we should cling to our faith, even and especially when we become helpless and dependent on another. Our dependence is ultimately on Him alone.

Yet so often, when we wait for lengthy amounts of time, the unholy darkness of doubt, discouragement, and despair may creep into our thoughts and emotions. This is especially true when we have moved from activity to the wilderness, or passive waiting. Our lives are eclipsed by darkness, and we truly feel alone.

At first, we grasp the promises we know to be true from God—for our greater good, for the salvation of our souls, for eternity. But, as time continues and no visible change occurs in our state of waiting, we begin to question these truths, as if they were merely delusions of grandeur. It is trying to wait for a long time in the nothingness of life.

The enemy preys upon us when we are stripped of our independence, our pride, and even our sensible faculties. In our weakness, we become targets for doubt, despair, and despondency. It begins in the mind with thoughts of hopelessness related to our helpless state, and if they are not immediately combated, they become a type of questioning of our faith—the very rock to which we have desperately tried to cleave during previous tribulations.

We are prone to these manifestations of darkness because we are incapable of controlling the outcome of our situation. Our plans, our hopes, and our dreams have all been swept away by this unexpected and unwelcome state of being:

> We are full of wishes, and our waiting easily gets entangled in those wishes. For this reason, a lot of our waiting is not open-ended. Instead, our waiting is a way of controlling the future. We want the future to go in a very specific direction, and if this does not happen we are disappointed and can even slip into despair. That is why we have such a hard time waiting; we want to do the things that will make the desired events take place.[46]

And what if our faith should continue to falter? Well, the final discourse of temptation for us is to despair altogether. That is why, dear friend, we must do whatever it takes to fight the enemy when we are unable to alter our circumstances or health. Print out Scripture verses that are encouraging to you and place them throughout your home where you will see them daily. When you encounter thoughts of despair, rebuke them with the Holy Name of Jesus.

Invoke the saints and angels, especially Our Lady, St. Michael, and your guardian angel. Even if all you can muster in these dark temptations is, "Please, help me. Do not let me despair," be assured that these heavenly intercessors will swiftly come to your aid. If you conquer temptations when they begin in your mind, they will be less difficult to overcome than if you permit them to fester into more sinister emotions and beliefs.

In the waiting, we must not become discouraged or afraid. Even if we do not have clear guidance or specific instructions on where God is leading us, we can be certain that the desert precedes deeper union with God and leads to our earthly mission. Ultimately, when we abandon ourselves to God's unfailing providence, we will begin to learn that our mission must be open-ended to whatever is indeed "best for us."

MISSIONAL LONELINESS

When I became a published author and public speaker, I had several people share blatantly with me, "I'm jealous of you. I've always wanted to be published." My initial response was, "I understand jealousy, but please don't be jealous of my life. My journey is different from yours, and if God wants you to have a book published, He will make it happen in His time."

Sure, that sounds nice and fluffy to someone who is "already there," right? But the truth is I have not yet arrived. When I entered my mission field as a writer, my life became more difficult rather than easier. Never before had I truly understood what it meant to persevere through the hurdles and hardships. There were moments when I second-guessed whether I was meant to be a writer at all. And the devil mocked me with either the thoughts, "Who do you think you are?" or "No one will ever read a word you write."

When we enter our mission field, we encounter a particular type of loneliness that was foreign to us before. Mine included significant time away from my friends and chunks of time spent writing instead. It meant increased sacrifices on the part of my husband while I holed myself away, writing out of obedience rather than excitement.

Certainly, our mission will be thrilling at times, but we seldom consider the reality that it will also involve more of ourselves—more giving of our time, more sacrificing, more loneliness. But what is this missional loneliness? How can we understand it in a way that is encouraging and renews our resolve to follow the path God has invited us to walk?

According to author and spiritual director Mary Sharon Moore, missional loneliness is "the interior ache that reminds me that I have thrown away all other options and have given myself wholeheartedly to a holy work where I am no longer in charge…It means handing over my plans, my need for security, my understanding of how things will be."[47]

Missional loneliness in the desert waiting involves detachment, mortification, and eventual contemplation: detachment from worldly and human love, clinging solely to divine love; mortification of our senses, will, and intellect; and eventual contemplation of God's immense love for us. Remember that contemplation begins our destiny toward eternity, because it is the only form of communication that bridges the gap between our earthly and eternal lives.

So, how do we move from our plans and tight grip on control to surrender in the wilderness living? How does our mission come forth with unbridled joy, with God making possible the impossible?

The old Christmas folk hymn "I Wonder as I Wander" comes to my mind as I write this chapter. What if we allowed our wandering in the desert to become a place of *wonder*? If we used the time spent in helpless, passive waiting as precious, solitary time to commune more intimately with God, would the wandering still seem futile?

We can intentionally choose the way we experience our wandering in the wilderness. We can be like the Israelites, who squandered their time worshipping false idols, grumbling about the miraculous manna that sustained them, and longing for the days of old. Or we can be like Moses, who, despite what appeared to be no change in circumstance, clung to the promise that God would lead them out of exile and into a place "flowing with milk and honey" (see Exodus 3:17).

That ache, that missional loneliness we feel in the desert, leads to wondering—to contemplation. It is true that each of us must follow his or her unique call in life, and that means God may lead us where no one else is going. He may, for a time, ask that we leave behind all the distractions and diversions that keep us from giving Him everything we have and all we long to become. But we know that missional loneliness, while a definite struggle, is also a gift that, if we choose to unwrap it, will lead us away from self and closer to Heaven.

HOLY TENSION

My childhood dream was to become a published author. From the moment I learned how to write using strange and beautiful words, I knew it was deep in my bones to express the pining of the human heart through written expression. Even more, I wanted to share with the world the gift I knew God had given me, one that flowed so effortlessly at times and spoke words of hope and encouragement to others.

I journaled daily from the age of about nine until I was thirty-three. These were, of course, private poems, reflections, prayers, letters, or thoughts that I wrote as a gift to God. With my friends, I wrote fictional poetry and teen novels. But the dream, once ablaze with clarity and a sure path, quietly became an ember as I "grew up" and realized that I'd never become a writer in the way I imagined.

And it's true—I didn't become a writer in the way I imagined. But the call returned to me shortly after my daughter Sarah was born. It was an odd tapping on my heart at first, rhythmic but gentle. The writer in me had never completely died, but the dream certainly did. Then, I knew clearly that the invitation to my mission as a writer was beginning to emerge.

The subtle tapping on my heart became loud knocks, and I listened to the Holy Spirit, though I didn't know where He was leading me. I only desired to obey and please Him, to do whatever was required of me, and I somehow sensed that it would involve a greater suffering than I realized.

When we receive a call that is as sure as night and day, we may want to jump at the chance to bring it about. Our well-intentioned zeal is often misplaced when we are finally aware of why God made us and what purpose He intends for us to fulfill while we are on Earth. The space between receiving our call and its fulfill-ment is what might be coined "holy tension":

> One waits…in an agonizing tension between hope and dread, stretched and almost torn apart between two dramatically different anticipations. A wise person will then steel and prepare himself for the worst; but the very tension in which he waits shows that hope is still present and that hope will often express itself…in the urgent and secret prayer, 'O God, let it be all right…'[48]

We might say that holy tension exists when a crisis or calamity hits, such as a loved one being admitted to the emergency room or following an unexpected surgery. During times of intense failure, expectancy, or strife, we may fleetingly experience this phenomenon known as holy tension. We wait with hope, but we also wait with fear. We dread the possibility of death or disability, and we pray with desperation that all will be well.

Another word for holy tension is "vulnerability." Vulnerability is that space where we linger between hope and dread, and we allow ourselves the risk of discovering either rejection or acceptance, loneliness or companionship, success or failure. It is agony to be caught in this place of uncertainty, yet the virtue of courage pulls us out of our hiding and into the center of what may come, be it all right or hopelessly tragic.

Somewhere in the midst of tragedy and the unknown consequences of that tragedy, we still find that flicker of hope burning, perhaps weakly, but present all the same. It's like that hope I rediscovered once I knew that God had planted the desire in my heart as a girl to become a published author, and it was God who had watered the seed, prepared me in the desert, and intended to bring that longing to fruition.

Holy tension does not mean that we maintain an unwavering certainty (though some do in times of trial) or a floundering faith. It means we experience something on the continuum between hope and fear, between a holy fear of God and His immensity and the hope we have in resurrection.

When we enter into the vast unknown, we might be like I was as a child: impulsive, ready for action, overzealous. It's because holy tension thrusts us from a place of passive to active waiting. We have been waiting without knowledge of what God's promise is, but once it is revealed, we excitedly want to bring it about with immediacy.

And that's the gift we have in waiting. It's the preparation for our hearts to be steady, vigilant, yet prudent. We neither hurry nor become stagnant, but there is a cadence of moving forward that keeps us going, despite the setbacks or mysteries, or perhaps in spite of the joyful promise we await. Our steps are revealed, one by one, neither too many too soon, nor too little too late. For God is the "lamp unto our feet and a light unto our path" (see Psalm 119:105).

Holy tension keeps us in that place of the present moment, where we do not succumb to paralyzing fear or dread, but we have enough holy fear of God to know that we must not stop. We must not look back with regret or long for the future of fulfillment. Instead, we must steadily pace ourselves according to His leading, never stepping ahead of what His grace provides us.

We will conclude with the wisdom of holy tension and missional apprenticeship from Mary Sharon Moore:

> It is so easy to think that God's calling is about tomorrow, about something I have not yet achieved, a way I have not yet become. Today, in fact, is the 'tomorrow' I could barely imagine, much less accurately predict, five years ago, two years ago, or maybe even last month.
>
> And I learn that apprenticeship to my mission in life allows no shortcuts. Every step, every lesson, every phase of growth matters… and is perfectly timed, following the necessary sequence of receptivity, action, and reflection that brings my life to unexpected fruitfulness and meaning.[49]

Expect the unexpected, for our God is not only a God of possibility: He is a God of *miracles*.

CHAPTER FIVE

THE SPIRITUAL BENEFITS OF WAITING

O Jesus, divine Gardener! We are flowers born in the garden of Thy Church and watered with Thy precious Blood.

—Archbishop Luis M. Martinez,
Worshipping A Hidden God

Many great spiritual writers have used the metaphor of planting and watering seeds in regards to individual interior growth. While we are waiting, winter seems more akin to what we experience spiritually than does spring. Yet we must remember that spiritual germination is a lot like the sprouting of a seed shortly after the danger of frost has passed: both take time. Both require us to watch, nurture, and allow the delicacy of the process to naturally unfold.

It's often difficult, if not nearly impossible, to see or understand the spiritual benefits of waiting when we are in the midst of it. This is especially true if we are in the desert and do not see a way out any time soon. Once the waiting is over, we can look in retrospect with fresh insight and realize that God was working and we were growing in some way all along.

This chapter will focus first on the metaphor of the seed, the sower, and the gardener as it pertains to what we experience in our season of winter waiting. Then we will unravel the spiritual fruits of such growth. Finally, we will explore the beauty of active waiting, or living out Advent in our daily lives through expectancy and vigilance.

Irrespective of where you are in your own journey, it behooves us all to allow the Holy Spirit to speak to us with renewed hope and confidence that our waiting ends with the gift of new life. It's helpful to visit these concepts while we are still in the thick of waiting, too, because we are better able to endure it without complaint or squandering the precious opportunities that waiting presents us. Let us begin.

Winter Waiting: The Seed Incubates

I'm not much of a horticulturist, but my oldest daughter, Felicity, is. If she had her way, we'd spend our entire lives outdoors. Each season, she exits the comfort of our house and enters this expansive world of possibility. The wonder sparkling in her little innocent eyes reminds me that, indeed, the world—even our small one—is full of new discoveries.

Whether digging up rocks and gathering sticks in summer or munching on the varieties of herbs scattered around the perimeter of our house, Felicity doesn't see inclement weather as a deterrent. It's more of an opportunity to explore. If it's raining, she requests to puddle jump with her raincoat and galoshes. If it's snowing, we must welcome the frozen tundra by collecting snowflakes on our tongues.

For me, the seasons each present unique beauty, but I'd rather live in a climate much like San Diego: sunny every day, low humidity, and about 72 degrees. Winter is an especially harsh time of year in northern Indiana. We receive all sorts of bizarre weather combinations, like freezing fog, a wintry mix (which means snow, sleet, and ice), and other interesting but dangerous manifestations of Old Man Winter.

I'd like to hole up and forget the world for about four months once the days have become so short that they don't really count. Morning after morning greets me with gray skies, no sunshine, and lots of bone-chilling temperatures. That's, in part, why the spiritual analogy of winter often gets lost on me—because I do not see the hiddenness, the waiting itself as a gift.

Winter waiting is much like desert waiting. We enter it with no visions or inspirations, no consolations or signs from God, no end in sight. We see no changes and only experience the bitter winds against our delicate skin. In the winter of our waiting, we cannot comprehend what lies beneath the surface of all we are experiencing. Everything seems abandoned, neglected, and dead.

How can we begin to recognize the seed nestled beneath the earth, cocooned in the womb of soil and incubated by the blanket of snow and ice above? We see the snow and ice (and perhaps even fall on it), but we can't possibly know what is happening beyond our limited scope of vision.

God's grace is the seed planted in us during winter waiting, but we do not understand what He is doing to us. The process of waiting is so painful! We'd rather run and hide from it all, because everything around us appears to be hopeless. It is in this winter time of waiting when we must learn to trust the Lord with whole-hearted abandonment, to lean on His bosom with no reservations, qualms, or fears.

Recall how we explained earlier that God often wants us to seek Him, which is why He chooses to hide in and around us. If it were easy to find God, would our love be sincere or complete? Probably not. We only invest our time and entire heart into something that or Someone who matters to us. Otherwise, what is obtained easily is often quickly forgotten and we move on to something else that captures our interest.

But, in order to seek God's face, we must understand the seeds He has planted and is sowing beneath the ice-covered earth. In order to transform our hearts from stone into flesh, we must permit Him to do whatever He sees as best for us. Winter waiting, then, teaches us to lean into God with deeper resolve and confidence and to seek His face in the clandestine places He hides.

Father Peter Cameron elucidates this point:

> Where can we turn to see the face of God? In our trust and abandonment, we await the Lord as the farmer awaits the great harvest that begins with the scattering of so much simple seed. He then goes to sleep at night and rises again in the morning, day after day, until the seed grows without his knowing how it happens. To claim God's provident

care is the Christian's exalted glory. That glory is the fruit of humility and confidence.[50]

Are we willing to patiently wait for what is in store for our lives, like the farmer waits for his seed to produce its harvest? If we are hasty in our desire to leap from planting to harvesting, we will miss the necessary growth in virtue that God desires for us to attain.

Winter waiting also teaches us to love through passion, through suffering and death to self. In God's garden, He waters us with the Living Water—Himself— which both refreshes us and allows us to grow stronger, that we may withstand the tempests of temptation and trial. In the winter, the Living Water is given to us in the form of ice, rather than the warm rush of fresh spring water we'd rather have.

If we truly long to be united to God eternally, then we have to allow God to use the winter time of waiting to nurture us through harsh discipline, the spring to prune us of what is excessive, and the summer to produce the fruit of the harvest. But we cannot produce an abundant harvest of love without suffering and death: "For love to produce its fruit, it needs sorrow."[51]

Are we willing to give God everything, so that we die unto ourselves? What will we possibly gain by our waiting if we shrivel up out of desperation and succumb to despair? God wants so much more than desperation from us, though He meets us in that place of weakness and misery. If we trust Him enough to die, we will merit the glory of new life in virtue, and our fruit will reach others with its sweetness: "Unless a grain of wheat falls to the ground and dies, it remains just a grain of wheat, but if it dies, it produces much fruit. Whoever loves his life loses it, and whoever hates his life in this world will preserve it for eternal life" (John 12:24-25).

Do not adhere so intently to the life you currently enjoy, so as to become hardened by pride and stinginess. Instead, generously give yourself over to the Lord with total confidence in His love for you, dear seed, so that in time, you will produce everlasting fruit for His kingdom.

WAITING CULTIVATES VIRTUE

While the seed that God plants in our hearts germinates, we continue to wait for the sprouting of a fine flower. But first, waiting with endurance (e.g., perseverance) will fortify us with virtue, particularly the theological virtues of faith, hope, and charity.

In Chapter 2, I explained that waiting produces obscure faith in us, that is, authentic faith which is not based on what we see or experience or even understand, but rather is rooted in sincere love for God: "Faith is the realization of what is hoped for and the evidence of things not seen" (Hebrews 11:1). The theological virtues, then, coalesce in a way that produces magnanimity of heart in us.

When we hope in God's promise to be fulfilled in us, regardless of how long we must wait for its fruition, our faith is concurrently strengthened, because we rely not on our senses to examine empirical evidence. Instead, we rely on our steadfast conviction that God will not fail us, no matter what we must endure in this life: "For in hope we were saved. Now hope that sees for itself is not hope. For who hopes for what one sees? But if we hope for what we do not see, we wait with endurance" (Romans 8:24-25).

So, waiting necessarily instills hope in us, because we are expecting that God will complete what He has begun in our lives—or that He will start a good work in us, if our purpose remains unclear. Through that hope, slowly increasing through our waiting, obscure faith replaces the infancy of our faith, as we strive not for what lay ahead of us in clarity and certainty, but rather have faith that God sojourns alongside us in the darkness of our hiatus: "Hope is trusting that something will be fulfilled, but fulfilled according to the promises and not just according to our wishes. Therefore, hope is always open-ended…Waiting is open-ended."[53]

Hope is what springs forth in our Advent waiting, into which we will delve a bit later in the chapter. It is essentially the hallmark of living our Advent call on a daily basis. And charity, the epitome of the theological virtues, is what we give to

God through passive waiting, our passion. Charity is the ultimate end to which we must attain in this life if we wish to spend eternity in Heaven.

Now we will examine the fruits of the Holy Spirit as they pertain to our waiting experience.

THE HOLY FRUITS OF WAITING

If we take a peek at Galatians 5:22-23, we will find the fruits of the Holy Spirit: "The fruit of the Spirit is love, joy, peace, patience, kindness, generosity, faithfulness, gentleness, self-control." These, dear friends, should be our beacon when we do not understand what God is doing to us or why. When we wait, we must believe without reservation that our fidelity will eventuate in some, if not all, of these spiritual fruits.

Waiting *particularly* instills patience in us, though each spiritual fruit will likely appear in some form or another as we faithfully await God's timing: "A waiting person is a patient person…Patient living means to live actively in the present and wait there."[54] Or, put another way, "Patience is power. Patience is not absence of action; rather it is 'timing,' it waits on the right time to act, for the right principles and in the right way."[5] Patience involves the cardinal virtues of prudence and temperance, too: knowing when to act and how. Part of how we learn to be patient is via seasons of waiting. If we are forced to stand still for a time, we become more disciplined in listening to God's voice prompting us when to act and when to wait.

Essentially, waiting produces perseverance and a more keen appreciation of remaining open to the potential of the present moment. If there is one aspect of our interior development that often gets thwarted by our noble and valiant efforts, it is when we step into the regrets or nostalgia of the past and grasp for what does not yet belong to us in the future. Both shift our inner focus from where God is speaking to us—in the here and now—to places that do not exist.

Only in the present moment are we able to value the gift that waiting affords us, a gift we would not otherwise seek or foster in our lives, but a divine gift nonetheless: "The spiritual life is a life in which we wait, actively present to the moment, trusting that new things will happen to us, new things that are far beyond our own imagination, fantasy, or prediction. That, indeed, is a very radical stance toward life in a world preoccupied with control."[55] Therefore, living in the here and now rather than in yesterday or tomorrow means we must relinquish control of what we plan and desire into the loving providence of our God.

This is why the aspect of trust is so crucial to our waiting experience: because abandonment to God's providence requires our will to shift from what we want immediately to seeing the current moment as our ultimate gift from God. Even in the silence of the desert longings, even in the midst of winter and passive waiting, we can discover that the quietude itself is our gift and reminder to slow down, listen, and be patient.

The literal definition of patience is "long-suffering," which fits in quite appropriately with our waiting experience, whether active or passive. Suffering for any length of time produces that perseverance, or endurance, of hope that we discussed earlier. Both patience and hope are present in the active waiting of Advent, on which I will expound later in this chapter. But the point of long-suffering is that the longer we wait on God to fulfill what He has already begun in us, the more appreciative we are when the moment of completion arrives.

We might also say that the "fruits" of waiting are produced by the Word of God, which is the seed planted in our hearts, as we earlier illustrated through the gardening metaphor; the seed unfurls and blooms for a short time (the springtime of activity and work), but it only releases its finest fragrance when its petals are crushed with sorrow.[56]

Here, we finally see the connection between the active waiting of Advent and the passive waiting of Lent: one cannot exist without the other. For most of us, this means we will undergo the more joy-filled anticipation of activity before we come to understand that what is required of us, ultimately, is *everything* through our passion and self-annihilation.

We will sum up the concept of planting seeds through active waiting and cultivating hope and trust with this hymn:

Wait when the seed is planted,
Wait for the rain to fall;
Wait for the restless green sprout,
Wait while the plant grows tall.
Wait for the coming Savior.
Wait through the heart's slow race;
Wait for the kingdom's dawning,
Wait till we see his face!

Hope when the sun is setting,
Hope through the dark of night;
Hope though the moon is waning,
Hope as we long for light.
Hope for the coming Savior,
Hope through the heart's slow race;
Hope for the kingdom's dawning,
Hope till we see his face!

Trust in the new spring's promise,
Trust through the summer's heat;
Trust in the dying autumn,
Trust through the winter sleet.
Trust in the coming Savior,
Trust in the heart's slow race;
Trust in the kingdom's dawning,
Trust till we see his face![57]

We wait in hope and trust. And, as we grow in both hope and trust, we learn the immense and inexplicable value of waiting with patience for the seed God has planted in our lives to sprout and eventually blossom in His garden.

LIVING OUR ADVENT EVERY DAY

Advent has always been my favorite liturgical season, but I couldn't really explain why I looked forward to it more than any other for many years. A friend, whose preference was Easter, once asked me, "Easter is the highest Feast of the Church and the longest season of the year. Why do you prefer Advent?"

Truthfully, my family always celebrated Christmas a bit early, peppering the festivities with an Advent wreath and daily readings. But the joy of the season in the midst of such stark contrast of the shortest day of the year and extreme weather fluctuations really appealed to me. I loved how the anticipation built each week as we'd light another candle on the Advent wreath.

It was only recently that I realized why Advent is so special to me, and the reasons are so expansive that I couldn't possibly include them in this section of the book. But the gist is that Advent, though comparable to Lent in the fact that we increase our prayer, sacrifices, and almsgiving, focuses on the *joy of birth and on the gift we have in our salvation*!

Of course, neither Christmas nor Easter would be complete without the other. During an online Advent retreat, I heard the speaker mention, "The law of the Incarnation is the law of suffering," which succinctly illustrates this point. We cannot have true joy without love, and as we know, pure love is never separated from sacrifice, suffering, and death.

How can we live out Advent in our daily lives, so that we "do not become drowsy with the anxieties of daily life" (see Luke 21: 34)? Unlike the desert and winter waiting of Passion, Advent signifies *active waiting*—or, waiting in community. Recall that active waiting involves the hopeful anticipation of the work God has begun in us, much like we explained in the meaning of the Visitation between Mary and St. Elizabeth. Our Advent waiting, then, calls us to be a Christ-bearer and Christ-bringer every day.

To bear Christ in a mystical sense includes undergoing "vocational pregnancy," which Mary Sharon Moore explains:

Pregnancy means 'to create a space for the other.' And at the very core of the anointed Christian life is this mission, to create space for the other, whether that 'other' be spouse or family member, a neighbor, a co-worker, or someone in need of my time, my gifts, my encouragement, or my hands-on compassion.[58]

In other words, we give birth to Jesus and bring Him to others when we avail ourselves to the promptings of the Holy Spirit and reach out to others through a sense of missionary zeal. In essence, we "create a space" for community, or engage in active waiting.

Recall, too, that the Visitation of Mary and St. Elizabeth was a specific example of this type of active waiting in community. Our Lady went *in haste* to her cousin upon hearing the news that she was pregnant in her old age! This type of haste does not imply impulsivity, but joy-filled and earnest excitement. Advent somehow moves us in haste toward the work God has already begun in us, movement toward the seed that has been planted: "This is always at the heart of Advent: that we are urged on, that we are hurrying, rising up, casting off darkness…[We] are urged on by a generous love."[59]

While we attempt to live out Advent by responding to our mission through community, we focus on the word "hope." The words "wait" and "hope" are often used interchangeably in Scripture, depending upon the translation. (I've found this to be the case especially in the Psalms.) It seems the two words are almost synonymous with each other, as we see in this verse from St. Paul's letter to the Romans: "For in hope we were saved. Now hope that sees for itself is not hope. For who hopes for what one sees? But if we hope for what we do not see, we wait with endurance" (8:24-25).

We could say, "In waiting we were saved. Waiting that sees for itself is not waiting. For who waits for what one sees? But if we wait for what we do not see, we hope with endurance." Do you see the parallel here? In order for us to grow in the theological virtue of hope, we must acknowledge that waiting and hope are somehow related, that we do not experience either by way of the senses. Instead, Advent waiting is akin to the obscure faith we explained in Chapter 2.

Advent waiting also teaches us about how we use the time we've been given: do we squander it or use it wisely? Let's revisit the parable of the wise and foolish virgins to understand what this means:

> Then the kingdom of heaven will be like ten virgins who took their lamps and went out to meet the bridegroom. Five of them were foolish and five were wise. The foolish ones, when taking their lamps, brought no oil with them, but the wise brought flasks of oil with their lamps. Since the bridegroom was long delayed, they all became drowsy and fell asleep. At midnight, there was a cry, 'Behold, the bridegroom! Come out to meet him!' Then all those virgins got up and trimmed their lamps. The foolish ones said to the wise, 'Give us some of your oil, for our lamps are going out.' But the wise ones replied, 'No, for there may not be enough for us and you. Go instead to the merchants and buy some for yourselves.' While they went off to buy it, the bridegroom came and those who were ready went into the wedding feast with him. Then the door was locked. Afterwards the other virgins came and said, 'Lord, Lord, open the door for us!' But he said in reply, 'Amen, I say to you, I do not know you.' Therefore, stay awake, for you know neither the day nor the hour (Matthew 25:1-13).

What—or rather, *Who*—are we waiting for? If we wait with drowsiness or frustration, because we do not see the value or purpose of waiting in our lives, we will end up like the foolish virgins. But if we wait with vigilance, the joyful anticipation of Advent waiting, then we will not be disappointed when the Lord comes to greet us.

The problem of the foolish virgins is that they assumed God would come for them according to their timing. They squandered their time by falling asleep. We often fall asleep in our acedia, impatience, worry, and daily distractions. But living out Advent constantly means that we wait for God's timing in our lives—which could be days, weeks, months, years, or even a lifetime. But we do not fail in our vigilance. We keep the Light of the World ablaze in our hearts each moment, so that we do not waste the time we've been given to wait for Him whom our heart loves!

The dark, desolate waiting of winter always gives way to the warmth of Advent joy when we give God our time, even when He does not seem to be opening doors or moving quickly:

> In the darkness of this night we await our Bridegroom, like the five wise and five foolish virgins. We do not fear that our lamps will run dry, for we come filled with the oil of divine Wisdom. We recognize the foolishness of attempting to live by our own ideas and opinions – our own false enlightenment. We carry with us the light of the Truth.[60]

So the metaphor of the candle of hope burning within our hearts bears increased significance during the liturgical season of Advent. We light our Advent candles each day as we pray our daily meditation. Each time we add another candle, the momentum of excitement grows within us. This waiting is not daunting; rather, it alights something new in us. The Holy Spirit stirs our hearts toward a greater love, a deeper longing for what is eternal, and we find that our own candles become brighter. We begin to illuminate the world when we reflect His light. And light always sheds truth, forcing the darkness to dissipate as we face this newfound awareness of ourselves, others, and God:

> We will find that [this burning in our heart] is like a candle within us. It is not a big candle. We must keep this flame alight, so that it burns through the layers of whatever we have put on top of it, and allow the expectation that is within us to come forth…We will become full of gladness, knowing that a great gift is about to be given to us.[61]

And that is the fullness of living out Advent every day. We know that God has great gifts in store for us, but the greatest gift of all is the gift of Himself. Therefore, when we wait with vigilance and acute sensitivity to God's murmurings within our hearts, we live out this joyful time without wanting anything other than God Himself. In turn, we give God more of ourselves, too.

The prophet Isaiah reminds us that waiting for God is never wasted time: "The Lord is waiting to show you favor and he rises to pity you; for the Lord is a God of justice: blessed are all who wait for him!" (30:18). The only folly of waiting is when we do not acquiesce out of charity to whatever God wills for us, even when we don't understand, like, or want what is happening to us. That is how Advent and Lent coincide within our waiting experiences: we cannot actively wait without dying to our own longings in favor of God's desire for us.

To conclude this section, let us ponder the beautiful Advent hymn by John Foley, S.J., "Patience, People":

> Patience, people, till the Lord is come.
> See the farmer await the yield of the soil. He watches it in winter and
> in spring rain.
> Patience, people, for the Lord is coming.
> You have seen the purpose of the Lord. You know of his compassion
> and his mercy.
> Patience, people, for the Lord is coming.
> Steady your hearts, for the Lord is close at hand. And do not grumble,
> one against the other.
> Patience, people, for the Lord is coming.[62]

GROWING IN COMMUNITY: WAITING FOSTERS A DEEPER AWARENESS OF OTHERS

Living out Advent, then, teaches us how to become more aware of God, ourselves, and others through this acute sense of community. When we are vigilant, our hearts are awake, attuned to the stirrings of the Holy Spirit as He masterfully brings about a greater compassion for the plight of the suffering. We cannot truly hear that "still, small voice" (see 1 Kings 19:11-13) when we are imbued with distractions and noise. Active waiting stills us both interiorly and exteriorly, so that we naturally grow in self-knowledge, as well as knowledge of God and of others.

What does it mean to become more aware of "the other"? Pregnancy draws the mother away from only thinking of herself to a perpetual desire to care for the one who is dependent upon her for his life source. Likewise, when we wait in the joyful hope of Advent, we notice the marginalized, forgotten, weary, and broken-hearted people all around us—in our families, neighborhoods, workplaces, parishes, etc. The "helpless person"[63] brings people together to assist the one who is in need through a greater sense of community and missionary zeal or neighborliness; in this way, the helpless person effects gratitude on the family or caregiver.

We may not consider every person in need to be helpless, so to speak, but rather only the one who is severely incapacitated, disabled, or elderly. Yet we all experience, to some degree or another, a sense of helplessness in our lives. If we can remember what it is like to *feel* helpless on an emotional level, then when we are physically unable to care for ourselves, we can better see how we, too, truly are helpless in this spiritual sense.

Because we live in a society and modern age in which helplessness is viewed exclusively as weakness, this state of being (rather than doing) is often undesirable, isn't it? No one wants to be dependent on someone else for care, even in a very mild sense of the word. I recall that when our middle daughter, Sarah, was born with a rare disease that requires numerous outpatient visits and surgeries, I entered that state of helplessness. I *needed* a community to gather around our family and chip in to do what I was unable to do: make meals, do laundry, clean, and watch our oldest daughter while I was away with Sarah.

Even so, I didn't necessarily *want* to be in a position of depending on others—possibly acquaintances or even strangers—to come into my home, my domestic domain, and do what I was "supposed" to be doing. But, in acknowledging my limitations through the lens of humility and gratitude, I accepted the help that God sent us through others. Initially resistant, one of my good friends from our parish said so succinctly to me, "When you decline someone's offer to help you, you may be denying them an opportunity to perform a work of mercy." That changed everything for me, and from that moment on, I marveled as God moved countless people who truly felt called to help our family in the ways they were able. It was beautiful to watch the gifts of the Holy Spirit come to our aid through neighbors and friends.

So, as I was contemplating the incredible importance of this new awareness of others by becoming aware of my own lack and limitations, I saw helplessness, or dependence, in a new way. It is truly humbling to be at the mercy of God for whatever one needs. But that is often how God gets us to a place in our spiritual walk in which we are able to see every human life—in every stage and phase— as equally valuable and *necessary*. It wasn't insignificant that He chose to enter human existence as a defenseless, helpless little baby. We, too, are called to be childlike in order to enter the kingdom of Heaven, which means we must become helpless and dependent.

In our helpless state, we realize that by becoming dependent on someone else for a time, we must learn to become entirely reliant upon God for everything. Helplessness initiates a sense of awareness—that we are not alone, we are not burdensome, and we are not called to be "useful" our entire lives. The necessity of our humanity resides in our very existence, the fact that we "are" rather than "do."

Do we consider, though, that the weakness of someone who depends on us is truly *necessary* to society? Many people would rather ignore or get rid of those who only "take up space" in nursing homes and rehabilitation facilities than to care for them with compassion. Here's where our focus must shift from activity to receptivity, however:

> The presence of a helpless person suddenly generates…a whole new
> range of possibilities – the positive response of attention or negative
> response of indifference, the application of good sense or the display

of panic, effective action or ostentatious emotion, skill or clumsiness in pondering help, hesitation, or impetuosity…It is in this sense that the helpless person becomes, in his helplessness, extremely important.[64]

Irrespective of how others respond to those who are unable to care for themselves, we must choose to respond to them with newfound awareness of how important they still are. I think of the people I know who are aging, and I see how tough it is for them to lose their independence. They often contest the help that is offered to them; either that, or they are riddled with guilt at the necessity of someone else becoming their caregiver. I've even heard it stated, "I'm so sorry that I'm such a burden." How tragic is it that we see ourselves—or anyone in need of help—as a burden? It seems to be more the case when it is us rather than others.

We can begin to understand and accept that helplessness is a necessary stage of every human life, that we are "extremely important" in this state as W.H. Vanstone says, and that in our state of dependence, we bring about some hidden goodness in others when they emerge from their comfortable lives in order to bring about that sense of community, of coming together in genuine Christian love and care.

Henri Nouwen expounds on this point: "Christian community is the place where we keep the flame alive among us and take it seriously, so that it can grow and become stronger in us. In this way we can live with courage, trusting that there is a spiritual power in us that allows us to live in this world without being seduced constantly by despair, lostness, and darkness."[65] In other words, God's grace is not lost upon our sense of despondency when we are in need of help. Instead, if we allow His grace to unfold, this beautiful sense of community—sorely needed, yet deeply lacking in our Information Age—draws people back to living their own Advent, a life of expectancy and joyful giving.

Passive waiting, for us, is likely so hard to experience because we become emptied of our egos. There is no room for the human ego when one becomes helpless. The childlike love that is necessary for us to achieve before we die includes spiritual poverty. It also means we must rely on God's providence for all of our needs in total trust and abandonment, as we've earlier explained. To become as a child when one has tasted the freedom of autonomy is often humiliating and debilitating, but only to the ego—not to the soul, at least not to the soul's detriment.

"Waiting can be the most intense and poignant of all human experiences... which strips us of affectation and self-deception and reveals to us the reality of our needs, our values, and ourselves."[66] The intensity and agony we feel as others begin to take over the care of our homes and families is essentially this spiritual stripping of self. When we become empty of pride, we see the truth of who we are and what we need. There is nothing for us to hide behind anymore. The stark confrontation of our neediness can lead us to despair, but it can also lend itself to hope—that space between fear and expectation.

Not long ago, I spoke with a couple who had both been diagnosed with cancer at the same time. They expressed to me how much cancer awakened them to a deeper appreciation of the little things, through what they coined as their "chemo walks." Every day, they would walk outside together and just pause in gratitude to all of the wonders of creation around them: the songbird, the colors of the flowers and trees, the fresh summer breeze, a sunrise, a cup of tea or short conversation with a friend, a meal. Before they became helpless in a sense, they didn't realize how many blessings were all around them.

Helplessness, then, draws us out of our comfortable lives and into a keener appreciation of what God has given to us through community. We see things differently. We experience life differently, in a profoundly fresh and new way. Therefore, everything we give or receive becomes special, because we are sensitive to the beauty of needing and receiving through community: "Through our awareness of needs we become exposed to powers and qualities in the world which otherwise would pass unrecognized...The awareness of need generates a sharper sensitivity or wider receptivity."[67]

What we can draw from all of this is that waiting offers us incredible spiritual benefits and opportunities to truly come alive, for our senses and values to be awakened or renewed, for us to stop taking for granted the little hugs and kisses that God sends us every day. We realize that living the earnest anticipation of Advent awakens our souls, too, as we strive to expect God to do great things in, around, and through us every day.

Waiting isn't so much a disappointment as it is a paradoxical gift. It's what we do in the midst of it, while we are living that waiting experience, that makes the difference.

CHAPTER SIX

PASSION IS OUR PURPOSE—
KEEP MOVING FORWARD

Have patience to walk short steps until you
have wings to fly.

—St. Francis de Sales

Two significant but separate spiritual epiphanies happened to me years before I understood that my own passion through suffering and trial would become the means of my sanctification. As a cradle Catholic, I understood the concept of redemptive suffering, but until the Lord presented it to me in a very tangible way, I didn't accept it as necessary.

Many years ago, when I was in the springtime of my faith and youth was on my side, I visited our local perpetual Eucharistic Adoration chapel every day to spend an hour of silence and prayer in Jesus's presence. On one such occasion, I discovered a thick pamphlet that described St. Faustina's visions of Heaven, Hell, and Purgatory. (Please note that this was long before Divine Mercy Sunday came into being, and not many people knew of St. Faustina at the time.)

Enraptured by what I read, I knew it was true: that the road to Heaven is strewn with rocks and thorns, thistles and brambles. St. Faustina saw this path, which was not aesthetically pleasing by any means, and on it were countless souls in various stages of suffering. Some were crying, others appeared weak, and some were injured or even dying. Some were being carried by others. But all were relentlessly moving forward on this path that appeared to be the cause of their destruction and pain. Suddenly, without warning, they came upon a lustrous meadow filled with lush greenery, clear and sunny skies, and beautiful flowers and birds. Every one of them leapt for joy and, as St. Faustina described it, immediately forgot all of their sufferings.

Passion—our participation in Christ's Passion through our own call to suffering—is the passive waiting that comprises most of our life experiences *of* waiting. Instead of seeing my path of suffering as the end, I started to see it as a necessary means *to* my end—resurrection, or Heaven. After reading about this vision, my attitude toward suffering began to soften just a bit. Over time, it would need to soften even more.

Almost ten years after this occurrence in the Adoration Chapel, I was in the midst of weekly spiritual direction. Ben and I had only been married about two years; I had lost my job as a high school counselor and lamented—in an empty house—on a daily basis that the house was so empty without children. We had begun the journey into infertility, and I truly didn't know if we'd ever be able to have biological children.

Part of my assignment through spiritual direction was to read *The Collected Works of St. John of the Cross.* Every day, I'd sit on our family room couch with my weathered copy and beg the Holy Spirit to enlighten my understanding of St. John's timeless spiritual wisdom. One day, out of nowhere, I looked up at a framed painting that was hanging above our television. It had been in the same place for years. Though I'd seen it hundreds of times, I'd never truly seen it with the light of understanding.

The painting is of a tempest in the middle of the ocean. It is nighttime. In the distance, there is a lighthouse with its light beaming forth radiant rays across the foamy sea. Behind the lighthouse are two outstretched hands, larger than life itself, in the position of heeding the viewer or perhaps initiating an embrace.

What I saw that day in the painting—for the first time—was my own life ahead. Somehow God communicated to me that the stormy sea indicated some tumultuous times that were coming. Since the setting of the painting is at night, it is dark, and I knew from reading St. John of the Cross that this meant the dark night of my soul. The light on the lighthouse was the beacon of obscure faith, which would be my only guide through the desert, desolation, and passive waiting. God's outstretched hands were beckoning me to enter into this holy darkness with full knowledge and consent.

Following this interior illumination, God spoke to my heart: "Do you accept the cross of suffering I give you?" I knew the question wasn't posed in such a way that God *expected* me to say yes. It was an open-ended question, one that I knew with certainty indicated an invitation rather than an omen. In that moment, I understood it to be God's merciful way of preparing me for whatever hardships were to come, should I say yes. But even if I said no, I knew God loved me the same as if I had said yes.

It was a truly free choice on my part, and after a fleeting moment of hesitation to think it over, I said yes. It was a yes spoken with full consent, full knowledge, and a deeper gratitude for God's gift of understanding for which I had prayed. Suffering, though arduous and deeply painful, led me to see that the cross was my call to love. Suffering through my own passion was the means by which I could be transformed by Love into a pure, perfect love.

THE AGONY OF EXPECTANCY

We briefly defined the difference between active and passive waiting in Chapter 3, but now is the time to delve more comprehensively into the mystery of passion and why it is the ultimate means for us to accomplish before we enter Heaven. We will call this the "agony of expectancy,"[68] because our agony leads us to the expectation of resurrection through the redemption of Christ.

It seems that passive waiting is so disdainful to many, because we have at least subconsciously adopted the societal mindset that God is somehow *always* moving (never resting or waiting), *always* autonomous (never dependent), and therefore entirely irrelevant to our times of passive waiting. Let's stick with the paradox of "agony of expectancy." The truth is that God is always *both* moving and waiting, as well as both perfectly autonomous yet helpless. We see the passion of God through the Person of Jesus. In His dependency, through His exposure to being handed over into the hands of wicked men, we understand that God has become *one of us*.

W.H. Vanstone elaborates, "The popular imagination discerns nothing in God: no dependence, no waiting, no exposure, nothing of passion or possibility... and therefore, when these conditions appear in the life of man, they must appear fundamentally 'ungodlike;' and therefore again they must appear alien to the proper status of man and unworthy of his unique dignity."[69]

If we revisit the concept of why waiting is so difficult (see Chapter 1), we see how working is far preferable to waiting—unless we contemplate the Paschal Mystery with the intention of allowing God to transform us when we are also called to be at the disposal of others through our helpless conditions or in circumstances beyond our control. Our passive waiting opens wide the gates of Jesus's mercy when we unite these little and large crosses with His suffering and death.

In order to begin to live our own passion and understand why it is vital to our eternal life with God in Heaven, we have to change our attitude toward it. We have to see Jesus once again as a tiny infant, totally defenseless and completely trusting of His mother to nurture Him. Human dignity can be reclaimed through passive waiting if we remember that helplessness is not inferior to independence: "Either this dependence and limitation must be a source of increasing resentment and frustration and even self-contempt; or there must be a rediscovery of the dignity which belongs to man as patient, as object, as one who waits upon the world and receives that which is done to him."[70]

Recall how we earlier explained that Jesus moved from being the subject of His life (activity, or active waiting when His ministry flourished) to being the object of what was done to Him (passive waiting, or being handed over). This occurred in the Garden of Gethsemane, when Judas betrayed Him. But before this "passibility" came to fruition, Jesus said something very revealing at the Last Supper that foretold the significance of His Passion.

At the Last Supper, Jesus said, "All *things* are now completed," but on the Cross He said, "*It* is completed." What does this mean? It means that before He was handed over (e.g., entered into passive waiting), He told His disciples that His *work* was finished. Yet there was still more to be done. What was that? His suffering and death. Only right before He expired did He proclaim, "It is finished." This means that the completion of our life is not contingent upon our work or ability to contribute to society through activity. Rather, the completion of our life, the conclusion of what we were meant to do on Earth before we die and thus enter into our eternal reward, is to undergo this "passibility," or this passive waiting. There is "something beyond work that is necessary to the completion of Jesus' function or mission or calling: 'passion.'"[71]

Before I lost my beloved job as a high school counselor, before Ben and I entered the "passibility" of infertility (as we waited to see what God would do through our doctors and over time), I saw work as the epitome of a happy, successful person. My ability to do great things meant that I had to be involved in a myriad of social, academic, and spiritual endeavors. I thought that my worth was reliant upon doing God's work through volunteering for various parish ministries, achieving awards and accolades in my professional field, and taking care of myself and others with alacrity and resolve.

Even as a child, this idea of activity as being the ultimate goal to seek was reinforced time and again. I was a highly scholarly child, so the reward of straight As meant that I often was honored at academic banquets or the recipient of "model student" awards in particular subject areas. I raced past other students by overachieving. I studied hard and memorized everything—even marginal details that we weren't expected to know. My reward for that was testing out of "lower level" classes and into the "honors" courses, which, of course, were considered elite.

Outside of academic achievements, I won countless awards for my artwork, poetry, and prose. Year after year, my hard work ethic was validated through exclusive galas, recognition in plaques, or publications of my work. I didn't know anything else other than worldly success. It seemed to be what made my life of value—what I accomplished rather than who I was as a person.

So I saw myself through the lens of my accomplishments. I saw myself through the world's eyes, and we all tend to do that from time to time. It was only after God began to strip my life of what I was attached to, which included my school counselor job, rewards and recognition in the community, and my volunteer work, that I descended through these humiliating condescensions and wondered what my *real* identity was.

During this time, a close friend of mine who was entering the convent as a postulant in a different state said to me, "Make sure you are doing God's *will*, not necessarily God's *work*." Up until that time, God's will was the same as His work according to my perspective! I was incapable of differentiating between the two. But when I failed, over and over, at my efforts toward success, I realized there must be more to life that gives it meaning than activity and constant achievements. But what was it?

The Passion. *My* passion. *Your* passion. We cannot begin to do God's will until we allow ourselves to be at His disposal, often through the "handing over" from others, perhaps from our mistakes and failures. This is the crux of what it means to surrender, or rather, to fully abandon ourselves to God's loving providence. In passive waiting, when we long for resurrection yet must endure the pain of purification, we await without explanation and without end in sight what God permits to befall us.

Living in the mystery of passive waiting can be incredibly dark and cause us to fear, fret, or fight the struggle we encounter. This struggle is not one of the Spirit, but of our flesh fighting against the Holy Spirit. It's difficult to hear the message that God's promise will be fulfilled in our lives, because we cannot see it on the horizon. Yet this is precisely why it's so important for us to fall into God's arms, or abandon ourselves to His disposal in total trust. We learn the power of love by way of helplessness, sacrifice, and eventually obedience:

> To abandon oneself to another terrifies us. We feel powerless, defenseless. Yet, God himself has chosen to redeem the world through a powerless act. The will of the Father is not revealed through a powerful display of glory but through a powerless act. Jesus' death is God's answer. The fulfillment of the promise…is not as imagined. Through a repulsive death comes new life.[72]

It is in the terror of plunging ourselves into the abyss of mystery that we begin to understand true, unbridled abandonment into God's care. Living our passion through passive waiting reminds us that spiritual weakness is, in fact, what God uses to glorify Himself—as He did with His only Son, Jesus, through the ugliness of the Cross. We will not see the fulfillment on the horizon, and it will likely not come to fruition in a way that makes sense to us, but we know that God will allow what He has begun in us to come full circle and be completed. Our death to self is that beginning step toward new life.

What do we gain from passive waiting, living our own passion with purpose? Obedience: "He learned obedience from what he suffered" (Hebrews 5:8). What God desires most from us is obedience, even above sacrifices (see 1 Samuel 15:22). It seems that when we first begin passive waiting, we learn the necessity of mortification.

As our senses are eclipsed, so do we begin to deny ourselves certain comforts or pleasures or indulgences. These sacrifices lead us to understand that what we are moving toward is learning obedience. Therefore, suffering initially leads us into acts of mortification so that we eventually become disciplined through humility in obedience to God's will.

This *must* happen before we receive the reward of resurrection. That is why working, achieving, and constantly doing is not what God wants of us our entire lives. Yes, we know work is necessary, but it is not the be-all and end-all of our existence. It does not define us. It is not our sole identity. Rather, it is in the receiving, our helplessness, and our dependency on others in community and on God's provision that we begin our ascent toward Heaven. First, we achieve. Then we wait and allow life to happen as it passes through God's hands.

Do not be discouraged by this truth. It is not a portent of gloom. The sooner we see suffering as a gift, not a burden, the more we will accept—and even embrace—all that suffering can teach us. For pain is our teacher, isn't it? Pain brings us to our knees, begging for God's mercy when we are crying in desperation. So desperation is not our end, nor is passibility our end. Rather, suffering is the necessary *beginning* of our end, which is the new life of resurrection.

Keep that hope with you as you wait through your passion, which may happen upon you when you become a caregiver for a loved one. It may happen when you become old and infirm. It may happen if you are injured from an unfortunate accident. Regardless of how or when you enter your passion, do it with the intention of loving more fully and living through abandonment to everything God sends you. Then pain will no longer be an unwanted visitor, but a welcome companion in your life's journey toward eternity.

Let's reframe what we believe passion to mean. Some believe it means pursuing one's ache or yearning for creativity; others believe it means intense fury. But the word itself extends beyond pleasure or pain. It is in the waiting, the *what is done to us* rather than *what we do*.

The word 'passion' does not mean…'pain.' It means dependence, exposure, waiting, being no longer in control of one's own situation, being the object of what is done. So the passion of Jesus…connects with every experience of passing, suddenly or gradually, into a more dependent phase or area of life…It may be helpful not only to the person who is bearing the 'cross' of pain but also to the person who feels that he is 'on the sidelines,' that he has become useless or ineffective, that he is no longer making his mark in the world...[73]

Pass into your passion with the expectation of fulfillment. God never leaves His will undone in our lives, no matter how unraveled it may seem. Jesus walks with you. Walk with Him through your passing into passive waiting. Allow it to reform you in some way, to shape you into your authentic identity as a son or daughter of God. For you and I are more than what we do. We aren't useless to the world when we enter into a season of dependence. It is then that our lives become most important and necessary.

Jesus's Passion wasn't some unfortunate, sad situation. It was the fulfillment of His destiny, a reflection of His divinity. Only through the supposed weakness of helplessness was His divinity revealed. And why was this? Some deny that His divinity was based on the Paschal Mystery. But we know that the hidden grace in suffering is, at last, to love—to be able to love with no restrictions or restraints, to embrace the wound of the heart, the affliction of love that accompanies the sacrifices we make and what is done to us through passive waiting.

"Jesus entered into the totality or extremity of passion – the situation in which there is no limit to what may be done to one, to what one may receive or suffer; and at the great climax of the story, at the moment when He is handed over in the Garden, we see Him waiting, in the agony of expectancy, for whatever it is that He is to receive."[74] So, dear soul, the "agony of expectancy" is that we await love to be born through our trials and hardships. The fulfillment of our own passive waiting, of what is done to us and what we receive, is love. And that is what we reveal, as it has been revealed to us, in our own resurrection.

FROM PASSION TO RESURRECTION: THE FULFILLMENT OF WAITING

Perhaps the reason most of us dread meditating on, and living, the passion story is that it is filled with unspeakable acts of torment and agony, all seemingly without end. The more we enter into passive waiting, the less we are capable of holding on to the promise of resurrection. Without the fulfillment of this promise, however, our suffering would be pointless. It would be as the world tells us—without reason or value, something to be eschewed and feared.

But we know that suffering, or passive waiting, is not the end result of our lives. It may be the final requirement, or test, before we receive the gift of eternal glory, but it is only the means by which we get to the resurrection. Through passive waiting, we must learn to focus on this hope, especially when we are teetering on the edge of doubt and despondency. The truth is that resurrection awaits us if we remain faithful through our trials. And resurrection is the fulfillment of our waiting:

> The Christian conception of sacrifice is not concerned with suffering qua suffering; it is not primarily concerned with the toil and the worry and with the difficulty, but with salvation, with the fullness of being, and thus ultimately with the fullness of happiness: 'The end and the norm of discipline is happiness.'[75]

So, you see, dear soul, passion may be necessary, but it is not the ultimate end for which we strive. Spiritual discipline is indispensable in order that we achieve perfection, and passion certainly disciplines us from every possible angle: spiritually, emotionally, mentally, and physically. True happiness is not attained by pursuing our own plans, as we have learned, but only by remaining faithful to God's commandments. We heed them out of love for Him, and He grants us utter happiness in return.

If working leads to waiting, and waiting leads to loving, then it is in the fulfillment of love that we experience resurrection: "We discover in the awareness of waiting the awareness of loving."[76] Love does not seek its own happiness; love seeks the good of the beloved. In the case of a life's work complete, love—in its purest form—seeks only to please God with every breath and possibility of being.

Love leads us to experience suffering not as drudgery, but as meritorious, glorious, and a rich treasure of spiritual gain. "In the perspective of one who has begun to love, the earlier freedom, detachment, and independence become of no account, and the loss of them appears as gain."[77] In the ecstasy of love, one loses the attachment to his former way of life, including his work and autonomy. If he is destined to be helpless, so be it. If he is destined to be at the mercy of God and of others, may it be done.

He abdicates the reign of control over this life into God's providential care. The surrender leads to the totality of freedom and, ironically, liberates his soul in this state of dependence when his former independent way of living had kept him captive to his attachments. Somehow, as he approaches the fulfillment of waiting through resurrection, he begins to love his life the way it has played out, which is not necessarily the way he would have preferred it to play out.

Life, then, becomes a "new dimension of 'glorious' possibility,"[78] in which he embraces both the good and the bad, the sorrow and the joys, the hidden moments of wonder and awe, the excruciating pain, the loneliness, the holy tension—all of it. Everything we have pointed out up until this point coalesces into this existential expression of holy surrender, which leads him to true freedom.

I'll never forget watching my grandfather die. He had been a man who enjoyed all of the pleasures of life and was very specific about how and where he wanted to die. His independence had been completely and cruelly stripped from him, which he struggled to accept as reality. But once he did, I saw relief in his face. I saw the exasperation from fighting his destiny of passion to resurrection melt away into oblivion. He was truly at the mercy of those who cared for him.

Even more, my grandfather seemed to gain a depth of wisdom I had never before noticed when he lived the way he wanted to. As he was dying, I saw the pain in his eyes, but it was transformed into love. His smile became peaceful, resigned. When one is bedridden and cannot feed, bathe, or clothe himself, what matters most becomes sorely evident. Yet my grandfather learned that he could catch glimpses of his resurrection even in the midst of his passive waiting.

That's what we learn when we finally reach the beginning of our end in life: that passive waiting leads us to a pure love, a sacrificial offering of oneself, and this is, in fact, a form of active waiting. There is a particular level of activity in our sacrificial loving, though we remain open and willing to accept whatever happens to us: good or ill, rejection or acceptance. In essence, we are "exposing ourselves to receive from those hands the triumph or tragedy of our own endeavor,"[79] just as Jesus Himself did when He walked the road to Calvary after being handed over in the Garden of Gethsemane.

Our resurrection is fulfilled once we have completed our own passion. We may discover there are many occasions in our lives when we enter into passive waiting, but only for brief periods of time. As we grow spiritually, we find that passive waiting becomes more lengthy in duration and intense in its affliction on us. Suffice it to say that before we die, our passion will reach its greatest apex. Yet, at its pinnacle, we finally see the glory of God. We recognize the strength in Jesus's apparent weakness, and our salvation is awaiting us while we suffer.

That is the epitome of our hope, isn't it? To view our new life in Christ on the horizon before the time of fulfillment. Somehow, suffering itself is transformed into love, so that what remains is not the pain we feel in our bodies or minds, but only love. A heart that loves completely is ready to meet the One who welcomes us with, "Well done, my good and faithful servant" (see Matthew 25:21).

Henri Nouwen offers us deeper insight into this paradoxical phenomenon of experiencing resurrection in the midst of our passive waiting:

> Suddenly we realize that the glory of God, the divinity of God, bursts through in Jesus' passion precisely when he is most victimized. So new life becomes visible not only in the resurrection on the third day, but already in the passion, in the being handed over. Why? Because it is in the passion that the fullness of God's love shines through. It is supremely a waiting love, a love that does not seek control.[80]

Letting go, then, is a necessary and beautiful outcome of seeking resurrection. If we truly seek new life, one that is bereft of anguish and full of eternal happiness, then we must first learn the art of letting go of control. We have to offer our yes to God, enter into whatever waiting He determines is best for our souls, and surrender to the process of pain. Our cross transforms us when we walk alongside Jesus. And, even as He struggled, He reveals to us what love requires, which is everything.

Whenever we are tempted to doubt that suffering reveals love, we may remember the Scripture, "My grace is sufficient for you, for power is made perfect in weakness" (2 Corinthians 12:9). We are made strong through and by the Cross, just as the Father granted Jesus heavenly strength on his journey to Calvary. Waiting with Jesus at the foot of the Cross reveals our true character and our strength in Him.

Applying Our Waiting Experiences to Everyday Living

What we have learned so far about the beauty and benefits of waiting is all well and good (and hopefully spiritually enriching), but what do we do with it all? How do we apply the knowledge to practical principles in our everyday lives?

To begin, let's remember that most of our waiting involves passive waiting—what is done to us, perhaps circumstantially or waiting for another person's response to something we've requested or asked. Think about times when you are put on hold during an important phone call, or when you are awaiting test results over a holiday or weekend. Even small situations in which we are forced to wait—road construction, a traffic jam, or long lines at the grocery store, for example—are opportunities for us to apply what we've learned so far.

Since passive waiting comprises most of what we experience, think about how you might be able to offer up your frustration or impatience silently, without complaint. Hand your sufferings over to Jesus and unite them to the Cross if your struggle is prolonged or uncertain. When you are in a situation of dependence, use the time to be grateful to those who are helping you through works of mercy. Be kind and patient with them. Instead of giving in to restlessness, use the time you have while recuperating to pray and increase your devotions.

Ask God what He is teaching you in the periods of rest and slow movement. Train yourself to live the message of Advent every day—anticipating the fulfillment of God's promises, knowing that your time of helplessness will not last forever. Even when we are temporary invalids, we can listen attentively to God's gentle tapping on our hearts. Usually, once we have recovered, we will discover that slowing down allowed us to spiritually mature in a way that we never would have anticipated.

Desert waiting implies that we are unable to see what God is doing with us, and we might feel tense in that space between our hope in God's promise and the place of darkness in which we currently dwell. It's understandable if you become discouraged as time carries on and nothing seems to be changing or moving forward. But don't get stuck in fearful paralysis. If you hit a wall with your mission and are constantly met with no responses or little visible progress, work on a different aspect of your calling.

In my case, I have several open projects in different phases, all of which I am concurrently working on. Sometimes, however, one particular project hits a standstill, and I simply cannot move forward with it for a time. Instead of getting discouraged or frustrated and then tossing my hands up in defeat, I pick up another project and continue to put small, but measurable, pieces together that lead me closer to completing it.

Regardless of where we are in the midst of waiting—actively waiting for a promise to come to fruition, on hold in the dark desolation, or passively waiting in a state of dependence on circumstances to change—the key is that we remain obedient to whatever God wills for us in the *present moment*. If we are always open and receptive to His beckoning, our interior peace will not be disturbed: "We can learn to be obedient people who do not always try to go back to the action but who recognize the fulfillment of our deepest humanity in passion, in waiting."[81]

Perhaps there are more, even better, methods you can conjure as you ponder these principles. Here is a formula I came up with that is simple and easy to memorize as you take to prayer what God is specifically trying to teach you in your waiting experiences:

Listen

If nothing else, waiting teaches us to listen, both receptively and attentively. It's important to prioritize listening above all other aspects of our spiritual principles, because listening wholeheartedly leads us to the subsequent depth of ongoing communication with God.

Listen in silence and retreat often into the cell of your heart. You can do this anywhere, believe it or not—on a busy city street, in the midst of your work day, while watching your kids play sports, as you are vacuuming the house. The recesses of your heart are where God waits for you to come to Him. If you do this often, even in little conversations, He will respond in a most intimate way, heart-to-heart.

In order to discipline ourselves to listen often and well, we should set aside times in our day for solitude and a sacred space for quiet. Listening takes practice and time, but it is an essential component of growing in holiness while we wait on the Lord.

Ponder

Remember how our Blessed Mother "pondered these things in her heart"? Pondering always follows listening. Our Lady was both open and receptive to God's call for her life, despite the impediments she knew would happen along the way. Pondering is closely linked with listening, in that silence leads us to both.

Empty your thoughts of its mental clutter and simply be open to how God is speaking to you before you speak to Him. When you hear His message—and you will, even if it takes several minutes—ponder what He is telling or asking you. Sometimes a Scripture verse will come to you, at other times a simple word or phrase, even a hymn or newfound spiritual revelation or insight. Ponder—contemplate—the profundity of God as you remain in His awesome presence.

Pray

Pondering, of course, naturally segues into prayer. At times, you might be inclined to recite the Rosary. Maybe your pondering leads to an inspiration in looking up that Scripture verse that came to mind. There will be moments you might scratch your head in bewilderment, thinking, "Why would praying a Divine Mercy chaplet now be so important?" Don't question this too long. Instead, be obedient to the musings of the Holy Spirit, which will grow stronger and more prominent as you practice this.

Spontaneous prayer, too, might result from your listening and pondering. Maybe it's a heartfelt outpouring of your intimate thoughts and feelings to God. It might also be praise, thanksgiving, lamentation, or petition—even a combination of these. You may be convicted to call upon the intercession of a particular saint, too. The point is, pray. Let your heart be the means by which you learn to be in constant conversation with the One who led you to wait for Him and seek Him in the waiting.

Prepare

Each of us is given specific gifts of the Holy Spirit at our Baptism, which are strengthened when we are confirmed. It often takes many years before we become aware of these gifts and how to properly use them for God's glory. At first, using our gifts may seem a bit awkward and unnatural, but prayer often draws us away from ourselves and into a greater certainty that we are to go back from contemplation and into community once again.

Be prepared for how God might be calling you to act once your period of waiting ceases. Try not to impulsively or zealously begin without proper preparation. God's form of preparation is often not what we would assume. It's not predictable or calculated. It's very much contingent upon our constancy in obeying what He asks of us.

In this stage, you might need a good spiritual director, whether lay or religious. If a call or mission seems very specific or grand and you don't know if it's truly a call from the Lord or not, seek spiritual counsel from someone you know and trust, or at least someone who is recommended to you. Realize that preparation for what is to come—what's next—is often lengthy and painful, but in a different way than active or passive waiting is.

Act

After a period of careful spiritual discernment, your spiritual director may determine that you are ready to go forth with the call you have received from God. We all receive a call, just in varying forms. Not everyone is called to become an overseas missionary. We are not all supposed to write a book or share our testimony publicly. So don't be frightened or overwhelmed at this prospect of acting.

In reality, acting is simply responding in obedience to whatever God is asking of us. That might be as simple as calling a friend whom you haven't seen in ages, or sending a card to a homebound relative you haven't thought of in years. Plan to be befuddled from time to time, especially if you receive an invitation from God to buy a gallon of milk and give it to your neighbor, or some such seemingly odd prompting. Yes, you might risk appearing a fool, but even if your neighbor is perplexed, you have done no harm.

This is why spiritual direction can be beneficial, or even necessary, for those who receive very specific calls to action through their prayer life and trials of waiting. Acting, of course, is our last principle in waiting, because it is truly the fulfillment of waiting itself. Waiting implies rest and retreating into contemplation, while acting suggests that we return to a state of activity after a time.

Learning anything new takes time to sink in to the core of our being and really settle there. Don't be discouraged if you find yourself swimming in a sea of chaos and confusion after reading about the philosophy of waiting, because chances are, you are right on the cusp of a spiritual awakening or breakthrough. Continue to stay close to the sacraments and daily prayer, and God will make Himself clear to you one day.

Chapter Seven

Encouragement While you Wait

If we wish to receive all that God wants to
give us, we must wait to receive it.

—Jeannie Ewing

We all know that the world can be a terribly frightening and overwhelming place these days. One glance at the daily news leaves us wondering, *how did we get here?* And, *where do we go from here?* As we wait, whether it is an anticipatory vigilance to see how God unfolds the good work He has begun in our lives, or a passive waiting, in which we become helpless and dependent upon others, we know that the world cannot adequately and completely answer our longings to suffering.

How can we tune in to God without tuning out the world completely? Henri Nouwen offers poignant insight: "Jesus says you must stand ready, stay awake, stay tuned to the word of God, so that you will survive all that is going to happen and be able to stand confidently…in the presence of God together in community… That is the attitude of waiting which allows us to be people who can live in a very chaotic world and survive spiritually."[82] God doesn't want us to live in fear or hole ourselves up as reclusive hermits while we wait. He wants us to continue to live in community, to reach out to others in Christian charity.

How do we live this out when we feel we are stuck? If life seems to be at a standstill, is it possible for us to encourage others while we wait? Indeed, it is. It is not only possible, but it is necessary. Understand that your life will cycle through many different seasons of waiting, some longer or shorter than others. But each season will lead you to a greater depth of understanding that God is drawing you closer to Himself in the desert; remember that we move from community to contemplation and back again as God sees best for us.

I wanted to end the book with specific Scripture verses about waiting and hope, with the prayer that you might be encouraged by the strength and clarity that the Word of God provides us. In very dark and turbulent times, I have discovered God speaking to me through the Bible as I delve into the daily Mass readings during my quiet prayer time. Some of these verses will likely be familiar to you, but others will probably surprise you.

The main point is that reading Scripture on a daily basis is truly food for our souls. Of course, we receive Jesus literally in the sacrament of the Eucharist, and if we avail ourselves of His Body and Blood regularly, we will become people of the Resurrection in hope and renewed strength. But, if we are unable to get to daily Mass, we can still read the Word that is proclaimed during Mass if we follow a liturgical companion.

Encouragement comes from God in many forms. Perhaps it is through a song. Sometimes I awake in the morning and have an unusual hymn stuck in my head. The words of the hymn deliver a message for me to revisit several times throughout that day. That's the Holy Spirit's power working in our lives!

Sometimes God speaks to us through a walk in nature. Birds are very significant to me, and I watch them closely from my kitchen window or as I saunter around the block with my dog on a cool evening. Matthew 6:25-34 often comes to my mind as I observe the simplicity of the bird's life: the mother as she instinctively prepares a nest for her soon-to-be fledglings, the manner in which she gathers worms and other odd bugs for the family's feast, and how she quietly but contentedly perches atop the nest without worry or care. Each time I watch them with an expectant heart, I understand that God is teaching me a very significant lesson about His providence in my life.

We, too, may become vehicles through which God speaks to another person. Don't be intimidated by this possibility! When we are open to the promptings of the Holy Spirit, He moves in us to speak to others in very unpredictable ways. I have had conversations with people who share their hearts with me in a way that I know it was God speaking to me through them. At other times, I've had friends tell me that something very specific I mentioned struck them in a transformative way. Don't be alarmed if you don't remember what you said, either. If we abandon all to God, He uses every bit of our lives—every second—for purposes far grander than you and I can fathom.

And so it is with waiting, as we've discovered by journeying through the pages of this book. As you read the Scripture verses and reflections provided below, ask God what He is speaking to you through His Word. You will likely come across countless other verses that pertain to your waiting experience, as well. These are just a sample of what you can begin with as you listen, ponder, pray, prepare, and act.

To begin, let's visit the verse I mentioned in the very beginning of the book from Song of Songs 2:7: "Do not awaken or stir up love until it is ready." Some translations offer this similar message: "Do not rouse love before its time." What this is telling us is that waiting is a form of chastity. We cannot give away what is not yet ours to give. If we are to be people of true Christian charity, we cannot capriciously dive into the waters of ministry before we are fully prepared to do so. And only God knows when it's time to share our gifts.

As you read, allow yourself to be open to whatever message God longs to speak to your heart, knowing that waiting refines the gift of spiritual chastity in you. Then, when God determines that you are ready to give of your time and talent, you can hand Him everything, holding nothing back. Until then, do not rouse or stir up love until it is ready. Let the seasons of waiting refine love in your soul.

BIBLE VERSES TO ENCOURAGE YOU THROUGH THE SEASONS OF WAITING

Make known to me your ways, Lord; teach me your paths. Guide me by your fidelity and teach me, for you are God my savior, for you I wait all the day long. *Ps 25:4-5*

In this verse, we are actively seeking God through our times of waiting. We enter into a place of solitude and silence, so as to meet Him there. If waiting takes a long time, the Psalmist explains, it's worth giving God all the time He requires before teaching and guiding us along a clear path.

Sometimes God will illuminate only one step at a time on our journeys, so that we remain closely dependent on Him for our sustenance and protection. If He chooses not to reveal the bigger plan of your life all at once, don't be dismayed by that. Know that He guides you even when you aren't sure where He is leading. What we must do is remain faithful and obedient to His precepts of the Faith while solidly rooting ourselves in the sacraments. Then we know we are on a sure path and our waiting is not in vain.

I believe I shall see the Lord's goodness in the land of the living. Wait for the Lord, take courage; be stouthearted, wait for the Lord! *Ps 27:13-14*

Remember the Israelites who wandered with Moses in the desert for forty years? We talked about desert waiting in Chapter 1, and what was likely so tough for many of them was that they didn't know whether or not they would literally *see* the Promised Land before they died. Even Moses was not given permission to enjoy the Promised Land, though he did catch a glimpse of it before he died.

The Psalmist here is confident that we *will* see God's promises fulfilled in this life! On this side of Heaven, we are assured that God will reveal Himself after a period of concealment, so we wait on His perfect timing to bring about the greater good we know He wishes for us to enjoy.

Being stouthearted means that we are determined and fearless in our efforts to wait for God to reveal whatever is to come. This, too, is a type of active waiting, because we are attentive at all times to God's message, knowing He may speak in subtle ways throughout our days. Remaining stouthearted and taking courage also means we are constant in our waiting. We do not falter with distractions or doubts. We simply, calmly await the voice of our Shepherd, leading us to new pastures.

> Our soul waits for the Lord, he is our help and shield. For in him our hearts rejoice; in his holy name we trust. May your mercy, Lord, be upon us; as we put our hope in you. *Ps 33:20-22*

In times of passive waiting, we often request help from God in the form of a lamentation or desperate plea. Expectant faith allows us to arrive at a place in which we embrace that confidence of not knowing. We realize we are in the midst of a mystery, yet we are not shaken by that reality.

Instead, we turn to joy as we praise God for all He has done for us. If we look to the past and recall the ways God has shown us His mercy and love, perhaps even through seemingly impossible means, we are more apt to thank Him ahead of time—even before He chooses to answer our prayers for assistance in this particular matter we face today.

This is a situation in which hope is so necessary. It is our lifeline, in fact, that carries us through the passive moments, the deserts and winters. In the dark, hope is our light. And with that hope, we are capable of surpassing darkness with our prayers of thanksgiving and praise to a God who never fails us and will certainly assist us in our hour of most dire need.

> Surely, I wait for the Lord; who bends down to me and hears my cry, draws me up from the pit of destruction, out of the muddy clay, Sets my feet upon rock, steadies my steps, and puts a new song in my mouth, a hymn to our God. Many shall look on in fear and they shall trust in the Lord. *Ps 40:2-4*

There have been many times in my own life when I have felt I was on the brink of total despondency. In the pit of destruction, so to speak, my heart sunk so low that I truly felt it would never come out of its dark night. Remember that God does, at times, hide Himself in us for whatever reason; it may be so that we search for Him more diligently. It may be so that He can abide in us without disturbance. Or it may be so that our love and fidelity may be tested and grow through obscurity of faith.

Irrespective of why God hides in us, we know that our waiting for Him to rescue us from the threshold of despair is, indeed, on the horizon. Until He swoops in with His mercy and cleans off the gunk and grime in our hearts, we wait steadily for that moment of resurrection.

Here, we experience both an active and a passive waiting, perhaps switching back and forth between certainty as we move forward in our mission and uncertainty as we come to a halt with being handed over to another person's decision or influence.

The first step in waiting for God in obscurity of faith is fear of the Lord. This spiritual gift is the foundation that sets our steps aright and assures us that our God is a God of wonders and miracles. He will never cease to astound us with how and when and why He delivers us out of the pits of destruction in our lives. Fear of the Lord shakes us to a deeper sense of awe in who God is and in His greatness, while acknowledging our littleness and nothingness as necessitating our total dependence on Him.

Then, we praise Him with joy! We can do this in the midst of waiting in order to somewhat allay our sadness and fears. But we also do this when God comes to our aid and brings us out of our hidden times in the desert and back into His glorious light. We are ready for what is next. We await with earnestness and gratitude.

I will trust in the Lord, who is hiding his face from the house of Jacob;
yes, I will wait for him. *Is 8:17*

Again, God hides in us at times. We could also see this as resting in us. Be assured that He does not rest in a soul that is anxious or fretful, but only in one that will provide Him the respite He may want. This is, in a sense, what it means to abide in one whom we love. Abiding in another requires no words, only silent admiration and jubilation over the gift of love and of the beloved himself or herself. If God hides or rests in you, it is precisely because you are His beloved and have provided a refuge to Him in your heart, so that He may dwell there—silently but tenderly—for a time.

Trust in Him while He does not stir. Do not rouse Him. In time, He will rouse you and awaken in you a new stirring of the soul. That is how you must wait—with patience and not reluctance, with peace and not restlessness. Surrender your thoughts and every detail of your waiting to God, and this time of rest will not only be His, but it will also become a gift to you.

> By waiting and by calm you shall be saved, in quiet and in trust shall be your strength. *Is 30:15*

This is a treasured verse for many people. It brings comfort when one is in the midst of dread and hope, because it assures us that haste does not bring about God's greatest gifts. Only waiting in steady interior calm does that.

In our world today, we've become accustomed to receiving everything instantly. We hardly have to wait for anything at all, and when we do, we become agitated. We're all at least partially culpable here, because no one is totally exempt from the influences of our modern culture. Even so, this verse reminds us that holy waiting requires calm, quiet, and trust.

It requires calm because we must be at peace with who we are and who God is. We are content with whatever He gives us, struggles or celebrations. A calm heart is one where God can easily enter and interact with us.

It requires quiet because the extraneous noise from the outside world often interferes with our ability to quiet our minds and restless hearts. Then, the exterior clutter becomes the mental clutter that clogs our thinking with toxicity. Seeking simplicity leads us to appreciate and embrace quiet more readily, because we have allowed God to do some spiritual housecleaning in us, and what is left is a heart that is open and empty, ready to receive all of the gifts God wishes to bestow on it.

It requires trust because we cannot undergo any season of waiting without total confidence in God. Trust means that we know who God is and believe that He does not deceive or lie. He will not leave us forsaken or alone. If we truly believe this, we will wait patiently in whatever halting place we may find ourselves, no matter how distasteful it may be. Our salvation rests in Jesus's Paschal Mystery; in our human weakness, God gives us His strength.

> I see him, though not now; I observe him, though not near: A star shall advance from Jacob, and a scepter shall rise from Israel. *Nm 24:17*

Have you ever sensed something so certainly but could not explain it? I can recall a few moments in my life when I would bet my life on a particular truth, despite the fact that I couldn't really prove its validity. One such example was when an atheist friend questioned me about my faith, long before I ever probed more deeply into Church history, theology, apologetics, or even the Bible. I *just knew* that God existed. I couldn't offer a theorem or proof, but I was willing to bet my life that God was real.

Obscure faith allows us to see something with certainty, though it is not yet entirely clear. We know without a shadow of a doubt that God is revealing something of Himself to us, but we can't quite pinpoint it with precision. In Advent waiting, we see God is near, but He has not yet manifested Himself through the Incarnation. The Word-made-Flesh is not yet present physically, but we know He is with us spiritually. God is with us!

Our Advent waiting reminds us that we can, in fact, understand or perceive some truth without entirely knowing how we came to that conclusion. It is the spiritual gift of knowledge that operates within us, so that we know something without seeing it clearly. Waiting allows us to hold on to that certainty through obscure faith without needing to see the entire picture revealed all at once.

> Bear your share of hardship for the gospel with the strength that comes from God. *2 Tm 1:8b*

There's no doubt about it: waiting can be a real hardship for us. But hardships collectively form the splinters of our custom-made crosses, which then become the source of our redemptive suffering for the sake of souls, including our own. I like to think that we relieve some of the suffering inflicted upon Jesus when we bear our share of hardship.

There's no doubt that we cannot wait or suffer in our waiting without some source of supernatural strength. That is why we turn to God in daily prayer and frequent offerings of our weaknesses, sins, and struggles, so that we are able to carry our crosses all the way to Golgotha. And after our mystical death (and literal one), we are born again into new life, the life that waiting carries on its wings.

> For God is not unjust so as to overlook your work and the love you have demonstrated for his name by having served and continuing to serve the holy ones. We earnestly desire each of you to demonstrate the same eagerness for the fulfillment of hope until the end, so that you may not become sluggish, but imitators of those who, through faith and patience, are inheriting the promises. When God made the promise to Abraham, since he had no one greater by whom to swear, "he swore by himself," and said, "I will indeed bless you and multiply" you. And so, after patient waiting, he obtained the promise. *Heb 6:10-15*

Remain faithful to God. What He has asked of you may seem too great to accomplish, and indeed, you cannot accomplish it alone. As God brings people into your life or across your path, enter into the community He establishes for you, even if it does not include those you would wish or think.

Recall often the promises God fulfilled to holy people, like Abraham. Abraham and Sarah were very old when God promised them a son. Imagine how unlikely it would feel to have God tell you that your descendants would be as numerous as the stars if you were old and without any children at all! Though Sarah scoffed at the idea, Abraham didn't doubt it.

There will be times in your life—many times—when God reveals something to you that seems impossible. If your natural inclination is to dismiss the idea as completely ludicrous, choose to believe instead. Draw upon that obscure faith that does not see clearly how or when God will unfold His plan for you, but be certain that He will, in fact, do as He says.

Sometimes we wait for something to be fulfilled that has not yet been revealed. Even during the times when God's plans aren't known, we can choose to believe that He wants good things for us and will bring about a greater good from whatever we must go through to get to the fulfillment.

> Be patient, therefore, brothers, until the coming of the Lord. See how the farmer waits for the precious fruit of the earth, being patient with it until it receives the early and the late rains. You too must be patient. Make your hearts firm, because the coming of the Lord is at hand…Indeed we call blessed those who have persevered. You have heard of the perseverance of Job, and you have seen the purpose of the Lord, because "the Lord is compassionate and merciful." *Jas 5:7-8, 11*

Firmness of heart does not mean hardness of heart. We don't wait for God with hearts of stone, but rather with hearts of flesh. And a fleshly heart feels the agony of waiting, the agony of ecstasy, that is, the torture of being separated from God even temporarily through sin and our earthly existence.

If we recall the metaphor of the seed and its germination below the frozen winter earth, we can easily wed the concept with a farmer's patience. Fruit is delicate. It cannot be thrust into unpredictable climes without first being nurtured—

over time—to withstand the tempests that nature brings. We, too, cannot thrust ourselves precariously into whatever it is we want to happen now. We have to discipline ourselves in that long-suffering patience that teaches us to persevere through the trials of waiting.

But, remember, too, that waiting is a season and lasts only fleetingly. Like the farmer who awaits an abundant crop, we must cultivate virtue and allow God to prune us before we are able to enjoy and share the fruits of our waiting. This verse also reminds us of God's compassion and mercy. He knows it is difficult for us to wait, so He sends us glimpses of hope from time to time, in order that our souls might be refreshed and rejuvenated to carry on in the struggles of this season.

Do not say, "I will repay evil!" Wait for the Lord, who will help you.
Prv 20:22b

It's tempting to retaliate when someone has wronged us. I personally struggle with forgiving others. Even slight offenses can deeply wound me, and I find myself, sometimes years after the fact, ruminating over what happened. In those moments, I understand that the wound has not healed, as I believed it did, and it is due to my unforgiveness and lack of charity.

Instead of seeking restitution, let us rest in God's justice. There are times in our lives when we truly believe we are in the right to forge ahead with some sentence of justice, but God asks us to wait for His conviction instead. I once had a job as a high school counselor, which I deeply cherished. I put all of myself into this budding career and worked very diligently to be a fun, accessible, and reasonable school counselor. But I lost my job over wrongful slander. I found out that some of the staff had been making false accusations about how I was spending my time or what I was doing in my office all day, and in the end, I was let go.

Instead of allowing God's justice to unfold, I became angry and wanted those who needlessly ruined my reputation to be punished for what they had done. I didn't wait for God to help me, to be my Just Judge. I pummeled forward and defended myself to the school principal, who rightfully didn't appreciate my approach and wasn't convinced to let me stay.

In the end, I wish I had waited for God! Yes, it would have been far more painful to wait for Him than to take this matter into my own hands, but it would have also taught me the discipline of patience and humility. Do not let your own pride take over when you are waiting on God to deliver you from some horrific wrongdoing. Do not seek vengeance. As you wait for God, you will feel incredible blows to your ego, but continue to remain firm in heart. Resolve to allow God to defend you, and you will not be disappointed.

> There is an appointed time for everything, and a time for every affair under the heavens...God has made everything appropriate to its time, but has put the timeless into their hearts so they cannot find out, from beginning to end, the work which God has done. I recognized that there is nothing better than to rejoice and to do well during life. *Eccl 3:1, 11-12*

God created an appointed time for every detail of our lives. Even those small irritations in which you find yourself saying, "If only I…" or "What if…" are occasions that God permitted for some greater good to come about. This beloved verse begins with "a time to reap, and a time to sow, a time to weep and a time to laugh." Not everything in life that happens to us is supposed to be happy-go-lucky. In fact, as we've learned, most of what teaches us and makes us holy is quite the opposite: the mourning, the tears, the sowing.

And the waiting. Waiting is our mentor in this case. Read how God has made everything come together at the proper hour, and He has given us the capability for timelessness, yet we still exist within the framework of time. However, God exists outside of time. Therefore, we cannot possibly ascertain the reasons why God chooses to allow one thing to happen and not another.

In a way, waiting conceals our hearts from discovering "from beginning to end, the work which God has done." Like I've said before, God often reveals only one step at a time to us instead of the entire shebang all in one fell swoop. We don't know the reasons for this, and we may never know this side of Heaven. But the point is that we must learn that waiting is a gift, in that it teaches us to persevere, be patient, and trust in God for all things. As St. Julian of Norwich famously wrote, "All is well and all is well and all manner of things shall be well."

GRATITUDE AND ABUNDANT LIVING: THE ANTIDOTE TO FEAR WHILE YOU WAIT

A while ago, I had a conversation with a friend about the importance of gratitude. Most of us have heard, to some degree or another, how gratitude counters the effects of fear and depression. Some people encourage us to keep a gratitude list or journal and write in it daily. Even five points of thanksgiving seem to draw us out of our egocentrism and into a more Christocentric mindset.

No matter how secularists want to frame gratitude, the real reason it helps counteract discouragement and worry is that it teaches us that God provides for us. In His providence, He grants us all sorts of good things, both great and small. When we are intentionally thankful, we draw away from self-pity and regret and into the reality of what God has given us.

Our family keeps a gratitude jar in the house. Throughout the calendar year, whenever something happens that we feel is a gift from God, we write it down and place it in the jar. Then, on New Year's Day the following year, we take everything out and read it aloud. It is incredibly powerful and humbling to have a visual representation of how blessed each of us truly is!

In addition to gratitude, abundance is another word that some psychologists are using to reframe how we view our lives. For instance, instead of thinking, "I don't have enough grocery money," we might think, "I have an abundance of wholesome food each meal." Abundance is another way of looking at what we have rather than what we don't have.

When we wait, we tend to look at our scarcity instead of our abundance. Life is half-empty instead of half-full. Abundant living shows us that our cup is actually overflowing with goodness and graces! Maybe it's the little things, like a sweet but unexpected card in the mail from a friend. Maybe it's a refreshing chat with a friend over a hot cup of tea. And sometimes, yes, it might be a much-needed refund check to cover some surprise expenses. No matter, our waiting can help us look at what God has given us rather than what we wish we had.

I know that when I look at where I am in my own season of waiting, I tend to see the mess and unfinished business rather than the fulfillment of what has already come to pass. I look at the manuscripts that are half completed or in various phases of development, the responses I await from publishers, and the fact that many other people seem to be "doing" more than I am at the moment.

Prayers of thanksgiving, which are an effort for me, assist me in looking at what God has already done for me and through me instead of what hasn't yet come to pass. I am always incredibly humbled when I thank God for the little blessings of each day, because often the bigger blessings that I missed because of my interior blindness also come to light. Then I realize it's not so much that my life is lacking something else; it's the fact that I haven't noticed the riches all around me.

As you wait, do so without fear or worry or concern. Resolve to thank God each day for the flowers and trees, the songbirds and sunny skies. Thank Him for the person you needed the most, and ask Him to bless that person tenfold. Thank Him, too, for the success you see happening in other people's lives, even if you think you are still standing on the sidelines, waiting for your "big break" to happen.

Everything flourishes in its time. So do not rouse or stir up love before its time. Wait for God to reveal to you when to act, but until then, see your waiting itself as an opportunity to notice and relish the gifts all around you. Then you will see only abundance and not lack.

Conclusion

Any kind of waiting presupposes some kind of degree of caring.

—W. H. Vanstone, *The Stature of Waiting*

Life is full of ironies and paradoxes. In the beginning, we unfolded the possible reasons why waiting is an unpleasant experience for most of us, namely, through the influences of our culture. It seems that our impatience has produced a mass apathy, hasn't it? If there is one thing that saddens me to the core, it is noticing the indifference in people's hearts toward caring about one another, the world, and most importantly, God.

As we journeyed through each chapter, we unfolded many beautiful realities about how we can wait purposefully and peacefully. We learned the difference between active and passive waiting, defining active waiting in terms of living out our Advent and cultivating a sense of community. Passive waiting can involve desert experiences, times of desolation (which are highly beneficial to our souls), and dark nights of winter. Our passion is the final leg of our earthly expedition, which includes most of our waiting experiences—as a helpless person, waiting on test results or waiting in line, a sense of being handed over, and missional loneliness.

Our intention during seasons of waiting should be to discover what God is speaking to us through the loneliness and periods of little to no activity. Has He planted a seed in our lives that is visibly sprouting, or are we to patiently wait, alongside the farmer in Scripture, for that seed to peek through the thawed earth after a long period of germination?

How we wait is akin to *why* we wait. If we attempt to use seasons of rest as times of spiritual growth, then waiting is never wasted. We can do this by first listening to God on a daily basis by seeking solitude; then by pondering what we heard; next by praying about the word we received through Scripture, a song, or some other inspiration; then by preparing ourselves for what the next step is; and finally, by acting at the proper time to do our part in cooperating with God's will.

The final point I'd like to make here is about *why* we wait. At times, it is really almost impossible to articulate the frustration, restlessness, and utter hopelessness we may feel when we wait. It seems that the world whizzes by without notice or care to our particular plight. Instead of being part of the action, we watch on the sidelines, and no one notices. We believe we are forgotten and forlornly seek to alleviate the feeling of emptiness and nothingness that waiting often brings.

As I was reading several spiritual books that seemed to offer specific insights into the supernatural aspect of waiting, I learned that waiting connotes a deeper level of caring about life, other people, and the world than does activity. That is to say, the more we wait, the more it seems we care about what happens to people who are suffering. Waiting people notice more and are attuned to the social sins that many other people easily overlook. Waiting people are, in a sense, suffering alongside the persecuted, the marginalized, the unloved and unwanted, the starving, the depressed, and the broken-hearted.

If you have not yet been consoled by any of the concepts, Scripture verses, or quotes in this book, be aware of one thing: *one who waits is one who cares*. Yes, it's true that caring openly and authentically will hurt the human heart. That is because the purest love, which is from God Himself, entails immense self-sacrifice. The more a heart loves, the more it hurts, because it sees sin and suffering through the lens of mercy. A hurting heart, a waiting heart, is ready to receive all that God has in store for it, yet it longs for other hurting hearts to come to a place of accepting God's love, too.

"A person who views the world with indifference rarely finds himself waiting. Conversely, a person to whom many things matter will often find himself waiting."[83] Authentic waiting can only happen to one who is open to receiving the Holy Spirit's gifts, to listening to God first and then responding in whatever way God asks. Sometimes, often times, that means that following God's will leads us to places and people who are living on the fringe of society in some way, who have been judged or ostracized or ridiculed or left to perish without any form of caring.

Caring, then, is antithetical to indifference. Choose to open your heart, to allow the Holy Spirit to flood you with His love, because that is, in large part, why you are on this earth. It is not to store up treasures or work enough to travel when you retire. It is not to be comfortable and build a cushy home where you can do whatever you want, when you want. Life is more than self-fulfillment. It is about giving more of yourself away, and waiting teaches us to do just that.

So be encouraged if you are not a person of apathy, because the world has enough apathy. Apathy multiplies when we keep ourselves buzzing about with incessant activity. Indifferent people are too egocentric to enter into the awareness of others that waiting bears on its wings. Will you accept the invitation to wait? Will you view it as a gift from God? Or will waiting become, as it is to most, just another burden laid upon your shoulders that you "must" bear?

Do not be indifferent. The Lord calls us out of ourselves and into the world of struggle and strife for a bold reason: to change it. Waiting mentors us through our own personal trials, through mystical deaths and detachment from worldly things. We become people of character and virtue when we wait with patience, perseverance, and hope. Even if you feel you are a far cry from any of these, know that waiting will refine your soul in such a way that you cannot remain as you once were. You will be changed if you allow the gift of waiting to transform you. And then, dear friend, you can go into the world and offer others the treasure of your heart, which is the gift of faith that you possess—more strongly now than before you waited.

The longer we wait, the greater the blessing. Brief bursts of waiting bring forth goodness and bounty, but the greatest graces come from the longest droughts and darkest trials. Wait, then, with God, and continue to seek Him even if He chooses to quiet Himself for a time. Wait with others, too, when they find life to be excruciatingly unbearable and do not understand their helpless situation. Be the Christ-bearer and Christ-bringer to the elderly, disabled, mentally ill, and addicted.

St. Teresa of Calcutta felt a "call within a call" to live among the poorest of the poor in the slums of India. You and I may never enter a slum, but we are still called to seek out the ones among us who are spiritually bereft, who are dying souls and do not feel that they are loved. In a sense, waiting for you and me is merely a preparation, so that we can share the strength we have discovered in becoming spiritually impoverished ourselves with those who are most lost and lonely, forgotten and forsaken.

Think back on a time when you were in a season of waiting, but then it ended. What was it like for you, before, during, and after your life seemingly came to a halt? Chances are, you became aware of your needs and neediness in that desert of waiting, and chances are, you gained greater compassion for others' needs, too. Why carry on with the message all around us that practically screams at us to consume, waste, and keep up with the "American Dream"? That dream is a delusion of grandeur. It is nonexistent.

Why not chase God's dream for you instead? Look at the world around you, and bask in the wonders of God's creation. Appreciate with every fiber of your being the gifts of life and love. They are everywhere if we only pay attention! When our lives continue as we would like, when we are constantly busy with this or that, we seldom attend to the small graces that touch our lives every day. Waiting, however, wakes us up. Our hearts are no longer drowsy, but awake! And in paying attention to the world around us, we begin to care more genuinely about what happens to the world and everyone in it.

We can be "aware of everything but caring about nothing." The world, to that person, has no meaning, and perhaps life itself is of no use or value. To the one who waits, however, "the world...presents itself as mattering: something in the world has power of meaning."[84] Do you want the world to matter? Do you want your life to have meaning? When most of us say we just "want to be happy" in this life, what we are really saying is that we deeply long to discover and live a full life, a life of purpose and meaning. Yet we pursue everything other than that which will make us happy and fulfilled.

What if waiting brought you to the fulfillment of your dreams? It's true that God plants desires in our hearts, but His ways, as we know, are foreign to our own. The path by which we are brought to happiness is not exactly by way of roses and rainbows. Instead, the road to true happiness is filled with temptations, self-abasement, holy darkness, and, yes, waiting.

The saints—all of them—had to wait for God to fulfill His plans and purposes for their lives. Some had to wait on permission from their superiors or from the Vatican before they could proceed in founding a new religious order or building hospitals or schools. Many waited for decades in what we understand to be this holy darkness, or dark night of the soul. Some have written about this sense of abandonment and emptiness, as if God had left them to fend for themselves. Some felt that God had also left their souls entirely.

And what can we learn from them? Much, but in regards to waiting, we can learn that everything that matters to God and all that will give meaning and value to our own lives will require us to give more of ourselves. We give the most when we allow God to pluck and prune away vice and cultivate virtue in us through seasons of waiting. There is no other time in our lives when we are given such an incredible opportunity to serve God in a more mysterious, invisible, and painful way.

If we care about the world and are more aware of the suffering of others, we are people who wait. And we do not wait with impatience or imprudence. We do not doubt God's presence or guidance. We simply allow Him to do what is necessary in order that we exit our time of waiting as a new creation. Like the caterpillar that weaves its chrysalis and waits for what may come, we also have to enter into the cocoon of waiting before enjoying the metamorphosis of resurrection.

Let us not make the mistake of believing that the little things we notice are inconsequential. Every fluttering butterfly, budding flower, and gust of wind are all beautiful movements in which God speaks to us. "When man waits upon the world – waits even for things so commonplace as food or sunrise or the relief of pain – the image of God is by no means absent from him…God also waits; and it is in waiting that He invests the world with the possibility and power of meaning."[85]

Wait, then, with God and for Him. Know that the doors of possibility will open for you once the waiting ends. And God, who does not disappoint, will exceed your expectations when you wait with purpose in the interims of your life.

ACKNOWLEDGMENTS

Every book is a work of collaboration. I never knew this before I became a published author. But now that I do understand it, I would like to extend abundant gratitude to the following people who helped make this project come to fruition:

First and foremost, to my dear husband, Ben, who spent countless hours watching the girls and taking care of our home while I wrote in solitude.

After the manuscript was complete, author friends of mine offered to review my rough manuscript and recommended I send it to En Route for consideration: Dr. Kevin Vost and Shane Kapler.

Dr. Sebastian Mahfood was generous to extend a contract offer, so I owe him humble thanks, as well as my wonderful editor, Cynthia Gniadek, who offered powerful insights into improving the manuscript to make it more relevant to a wider audience.

May the Lord bless you all and encourage those who read this book.

About the Author

Jeannie Ewing believes the world focuses too much on superficial happiness and then crumbles when sorrow strikes. Because life is about more than what makes us feel happy, she writes about the hidden value of suffering and even discovering joy in the midst of grief. As a disability advocate, Jeannie shares her heart as a mom of two girls with special needs in *Navigating Deep Waters: Meditations for Caregivers* and is the author of *From Grief to Grace: The Journey from Tragedy to Triumph* and *A Sea Without A Shore: Spiritual Reflections for the Brokenhearted, Weary, and Lonely*. Jeannie is a frequent guest on Catholic radio and contributes to several online and print Catholic magazines. She, her husband, and three daughters live in northern Indiana. For more information, please visit her website lovealonecreates.com.

NOTES

INTRODUCTION

1. If you'd like to know more about Sarah's birth experience and her condition, please refer to my book *From Grief to Grace: The Journey from Tragedy to Triumph* (Sophia Institute Press, 2016).

CHAPTER ONE: WHY IS WAITING SO DIFFICULT?

2. Retrieved December 13, 2016, from http://www.returntoorder.org/2016/04/defining-frenetic-intemperance/, based on John Horvat II's book, *Return to Order: From a Frenzied Economy to an Organic Christian Society--Where We've Been, How We Got Here, and Where We Need to Go* (York Press, 2013).

3. Josef Pieper, *Leisure: The Basis of Culture* (San Francisco, CA: Ignatius Press, 2009), p. 44.

4. Pieper, *Leisure*, p. 45.

5. W. H. Vanstone, *The Stature of Waiting* (Harrisburg, PA: Morehouse Publishing, 2004), p. 49.

6. Cardinal Robert Sarah, "Meditation of the Day: Interpreting the Present Time," *Magnificat* (October 21, 2016): p. 305.

7. Pieper, *Leisure*, p. 33.

8. Vanstone, *Stature of Waiting*, p. 109.

9. Father Peter John Cameron, "Vigil for New Year's Eve," *Magnificat* (December 31, 2016): p. 464.

10. Father Tadeusz Dajczer, "Meditation of the Day: United with the Prodigal Son," *Magnificat* (March 18, 2017): p. 275.

11. Sonja Corbitt, *Fearless: A Catholic Women's Guide to Spiritual Warfare* (Notre Dame, IN: Ave Maria Press, 2016), p. 126.

12. Corbitt, *Fearless: Catholic Women's Guide*, p. 127.

13. Archbishop Luis M. Martinez, *Worshipping A Hidden God: Unlocking the Secrets of the Interior Life* (Manchester, NH: Sophia Institute Press, 2003), p. 128.

14. Martinez, *Worshipping a Hidden God*, p. 149.

15. Martinez, *Worshipping a Hidden God*, p. 149.

16. Martinez, *Worshipping a Hidden God*, p. 162.

17. Boethius, *The Consolation of Philosophy* (New York: Dover, 2002), p. 34.

18. St. Ignatius of Loyola, *Spiritual Exercises*, 5th rule.

19. Martinez, *Worshipping a Hidden God*, p. 65.

CHAPTER TWO: SEEKING A HIDDEN GOD AND RESTING IN HIM

20. Thomas Aquinas, *Commentary on the Sentences*, 2d. 15, 3, 3.

21. Martinez, *Worshipping a Hidden God*, pp. 113–114.

22. Martinez, *Worshipping a Hidden God*, p. 116.

23. Richard Frederick Clarke, *The Coming of Christ: Meditations for Advent* (2012), Kindle.

24. Clarke, *Coming of Christ*.

25. Cameron, "Vigil for New Year's Eve," p. 471.

26. St. John of the Cross, *Ascent to Mount Carmel* (Dover Publications, 2008), book 2, chap. 4.

27. Martinez, *Worshipping a Hidden God*, p. 118.

28. Cameron, "Vigil for New Year's Eve," p. 466.

29. St. Catherine of Siena, "Meditation of the Day: The Patience of Zechariah," *Magnificat* (December 19, 2016): p. 289 (emphasis mine).

30. St. Monica likely experienced both active and passive waiting. It was active in the sense that she prayed unceasingly for St. Augustine, with total confidence in God's goodness and mercy. But it was also passive waiting in regards to the length of time – decades – that she would have to wait before seeing her son's conversion.

31. Henri Nouwen, "A Spirituality of Waiting: Being Alert to God's Presence in our Lives," *Weavings* (January/February 1987): p. 11.

32. Pieper, *Leisure*, p. 46.

33. Nouwen, "Spirituality of Waiting," p. 12.

34. Cameron, "Vigil for New Year's Eve," pp. 469-470.

35. Nouwen, "Spirituality of Waiting," p. 9.

36. Father Donald Haggerty, "Day by Day: Prayer of Gratitude," *Magnificat* (October 9, 2016): pp. 133-134.

37. Thomas of Jesus, O.C.D., "What is Acquired Contemplation?" *Rorate Caeli* (January, 2013), retrieved from https://rorate-caeli.blogspot.com/2013/01/what-is-acquired-contemplation.html on October 10, 2017.

38. For more information, visit http://catholic-church.org/grace/growing/9grades/grade5.htm.

39. Martinez, *Worshipping a Hidden God*, p. 109.

40. I'd like to differentiate here between infused and acquired contemplation, which is a comprehensive topic for another book. Very simply, acquired contemplation occurs by way of one's will and through ascetical practices, but infused contemplation is solely initiated by God. It is a supernatural gift of grace in which the soul experiences total immersion in love for God and cannot be obtained by any spiritual practices or eremitical endeavors.

CHAPTER FOUR: FROM WORKING TO WAITING—
ACHIEVING OR RECEIVING?

41. Pieper, *Leisure*, p. 33.

42. Vanstone, *Stature of Waiting*, p. 29.

43. Vanstone, *Stature of Waiting*, p. 37.

44. Vanstone, *Stature of Waiting*, pp. 83-84.

45. Nouwen, "Spirituality of Waiting," p. 8.

46. Nouwen, "Spirituality of Waiting," p. 10.

47. Mary Sharon Moore, *Conformed to Christ: Discoveries in the Maturing Christ-centered Life* (Eugene, OR: Awakening Vocations, 2016), p. 112.

48. Vanstone, *Stature of Waiting*, p. 84.

49. Moore, *Conformed to Christ*, p. 91.

CHAPTER FIVE: THE SPIRITUAL BENEFITS OF WAITING

50. Cameron, "Vigil for New Year's Eve," p. 464.

51. Martinez, *Worshipping a Hidden God*, p. 93.

52. Nouwen, "Spirituality of Waiting," p. 10.

53. Nouwen, "Spirituality of Waiting," pp. 9-10.

54. Ven. Fulton Sheen, "Quiet Moments, Daily Inspiration, Feasts and Fun for February," *Catholic Digest* (January/February 2017): p. 93.

55. Nouwen, "Spirituality of Waiting," p. 11.

56. Martinez, *Worshipping a Hidden God*, chap. 6.

57. "Prayer for the Evening," *Magnificat* (December 11, 2016: p. 152.

58. Moore, *Conformed to Christ*, p. 22.

59. Mother Mary Francis, "Meditation of the Day: Being a Healing Power," *Magnificat* (December 5, 2016): p. 77.

60. Cameron, "Vigil for New Year's Eve," pp. 465-466.

61. Catherine de Hueck Doherty, "Meditation of the Day: Sharing the Expectation of the Blind Men," *Magnificat* (December 2, 2016): p. 39.

62. John Foley, "Patience, People," 1977.

63. Vanstone, *Stature of Waiting*, p. 55.

64. Vanstone, *Stature of Waiting*, p. 55.

65. Nouwen, "Spirituality of Waiting," p. 12.

66. Vanstone, *Stature of Waiting*, p. 83.

67. Vanstone, *Stature of Waiting*, p. 107.

CHAPTER SIX: PASSION IS OUR PURPOSE – KEEP MOVING FORWARD

68. Vanstone, *Stature of Waiting*, p. 87.

69. Vanstone, *Stature of Waiting*, p. 65.

70. Vanstone, *Stature of Waiting*, p. 66.

71. Vanstone, *Stature of Waiting*, pp. 72-73.

72. Father Jose Medina, "Meditation of the Day: Grace of the Holy Innocents," *Magnificat* (December 28, 2016): p. 423.

73. Vanstone, *Stature of Waiting*, p. 70.

74. Vanstone, *Stature of Waiting*, p. 87.

75. Pieper, *Leisure*, p. 35.

76. Vanstone, *Stature of Waiting*, p. 97.

77. Vanstone, *Stature of Waiting*, p. 98.

78. Vanstone, *Stature of Waiting*, p. 98.

79. Vanstone, *Stature of Waiting*, p. 96.

80. Nouwen, "Spirituality of Waiting," p. 16.

81. Nouwen, "Spirituality of Waiting," p. 17.

CHAPTER SEVEN: ENCOURAGEMENT WHILE YOU WAIT

82. Nouwen, "Spirituality of Waiting," pp. 12-13.

CONCLUSION

83. Vanstone, *Stature of Waiting*, p. 103.

84. Vanstone, *Stature of Waiting*, p. 104.

85. Vanstone, *Stature of Waiting*, p. 109.

CPSIA information can be obtained
at www.ICGtesting.com
Printed in the USA
LVOW07*0647281217
561067LV00017BA/281/P